The Law of Attraction

Unlock the Potential of Tapping (EFT) to Attract Success, Love & Wealth

Volume 1

Written by
Marilena Mocanu

Today:

I have given this book to:

Because your well-being is important to me and my greatest wish is that you find inspiration in these pages to achieve your dreams.

Signature:

Disclaimer

The information contained in this e-book is educational in nature and is provided only as general information. As part of the information presented in this e-book, I understand that I will be introduced to a modality called Emotional Freedom Technique ("EFT") which is a technique referred to as a type of energy therapy. Due to the experimental nature of EFT, and because it is a relatively new healing approach and the extent of its effectiveness, as well as its risks and benefits are not fully known, I agree to assume and accept full responsibility for all risks associated with reading this e-book and using EFT because of reading this e-book.

I understand that my choice to use EFT is of my own free will and not subject to any outside pressure. I further understand that if I choose to use EFT, it is possible that emotional or physical sensations or added unresolved memories may surface.

The information presented on this website, including introducing EFT, is not intended to stand for that EFT is used to diagnose, treat, cure, or prevent any disease or psychological disorder. EFT is not a substitute for medical or psychological treatment. Any stories or testimonials presented in this e-book do not constitute a warranty, guarantee, or prediction about the outcome of an individual using EFT for any issue.

While all materials and links to other resources are posted in good faith, the accuracy, validity, effectiveness, completeness, or usefulness of any information here, as with any publication, cannot be guaranteed.

The Law of attraction accepts no responsibility or liability whatsoever for the use or misuse of the information contained in this eBook including, but not limited to, EFT demonstrations, training, and related activities. We strongly recommend that you seek professional advice as proper before making any health decision.

Dedication

This book is dedicated to my husband, Fernando.

Thank you for your unwavering support, love, and encouragement throughout this journey. Your belief in me, even during the most challenging times, has been my constant source of strength and inspiration. I am profoundly grateful for your patience, understanding, and for always being by my side. This accomplishment would not have been possible without you.

With all my love,

Marilena

I would like to inform you that a part of the revenues from the sale of this book will be donated to schools in Romania, Spain, and the United Kingdom helping to ensure that children receive at least one nutritious meal each day.

**Sincerely,
Marilena Mocanu**

Table of Contents:

Table of Contents:

Dedication

Introduction

Chapter 1: The Synergy Between Tapping and the Law of Attraction

Chapter 2: Understanding Tapping: The Basics and Energy Flow

Chapter 3: The Science Behind Tapping: Mind and Body Connection

Chapter 4: The Law of Attraction Explained

Chapter 5: How Tapping Enhances the Law of Attraction

Chapter 6: Step-by-Step Guide to Tapping

Chapter 7: What to Say While Tapping: Crafting Affirmations for Manifestation

Chapter 8: Tapping for Specific Goals: Health, Wealth, Love, and Success

Chapter 9: Overcoming Limiting Beliefs: Using Tapping to Reprogram the Mind

Chapter 10: Daily Tapping Routine: Building a Consistent Practice

Chapter 11: Common Challenges and How to Overcome Them

Chapter 12: Real-Life Success Stories: Manifesting with Tapping

EFT Tapping Chart

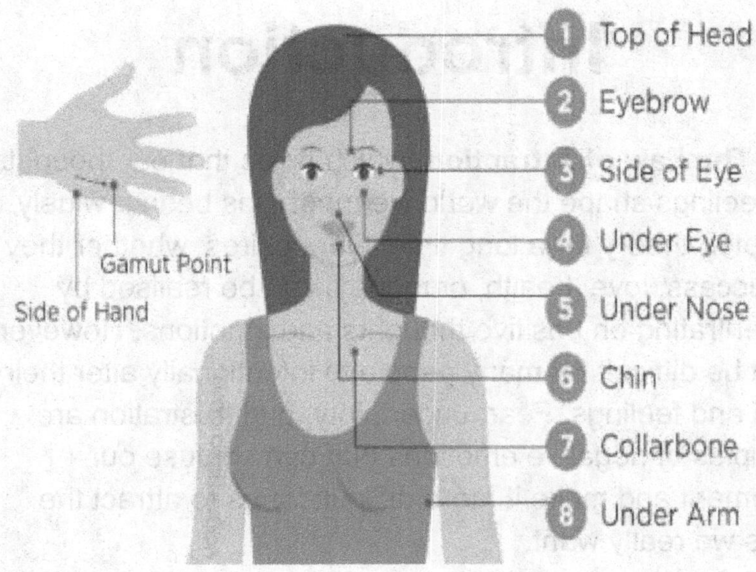

Introduction

The Law of Attraction, which holds that our thoughts and feelings shape the world we meet, has been a widely accepted theory for a long time. Our desires, whether they be for success, love, health, or money, can be realised by concentrating on positive thoughts and emotions. However, it might be difficult for many people to intentionally alter their ideas and feelings. Fear, uncertainty, and frustration are examples of negative emotions that can confuse our judgement and make it more difficult for us to attract the things we really want.

The **Emotional Freedom Technique (EFT),** often referred to as tapping, becomes an extremely useful tool in this situation. Tapping is an easy but powerful technique that involves focussing on negative feelings, ideas, or experiences while activating acupressure points on the body. By doing this, it dissolves the energetic and emotional barriers that prevent good thought and manifestation.

Why combine tapping with the Law of Attraction?

The knowledge that our emotions and thoughts have a direct impact on our ability to materialise is what links tapping to the Law of Attraction. In addition to helping in the release of negative emotions, tapping enables us to realign our energy with constructive ideas and beliefs, which creates an environment that is conducive to manifestation. You can fully use the Law of Attraction by conquering emotional obstacles with the help of this potent constructive interaction.

Understanding Tapping: The Basics and Energy Flow

Basically, tapping works on the same ideas as acupuncture, but without the use of needles. It entails lightly tapping on specific energy meridians—the channels via which energy moves—on the body. Traditional Chinese Medicine says that emotional and bodily suffering result from obstructed or stagnant energy in these meridians. By releasing these barriers and restoring a state of equilibrium tapping enables energy to flow easily once more.

The technique is simple: by tapping on key points—such as the side of the hand, top of the head, and around the face and collarbone—while focusing on a specific issue, you can dissipate the emotional charge associated with it. This creates space for more empowering thoughts and feelings, which are essential for aligning with the Law of Attraction.

The Science Behind Tapping: Mind and Body Connection

The efficacy of tapping is backed by both contemporary psychological and neurological research as well as traditional energy healing techniques. According to studies, tapping can lessen activity in the brain region known as the amygdala, which oversees the "fight or flight" response. The amygdala starts this reaction in response to stress or unpleasant emotions, which often results in feelings of worry, fear, or frustration.

This scientific basis makes tapping a powerful tool for anyone looking to improve their manifestation abilities through the Law of Attraction. By tapping while focussing on an emotional trigger, we are signalling to the brain that it is safe to relax, which helps to rewire the brain's response to stress, allowing us to "reset" our thought patterns. This allows us to release deep-seated emotions and beliefs that prevent us from manifesting our desires, in addition to calming the mind.

The Law of Attraction Explained

Understanding the foundations of the Law of Attraction is crucial before diving deeper into how tapping and the law of attraction interact. The Law of Attraction is founded on the simple principle that "like attracts like." Your ideas and feelings release energy into the universe, which will return to you in the shape of experiences and results.

If you think and feel mostly positive, you will attract positive experiences; if you are focused on fear, scarcity, or negativity, you will continue to attract more of the same. Our conscious and subconscious beliefs influence our reality, and for many people, the difficulty is in overcoming negative, deeply ingrained beliefs that prevent them from attracting what they really want. This is where tapping becomes essential in removing those obstacles.

How Tapping Enhances the Law of Attraction

The concept that our emotions serve as magnets for the things we draw into our lives is one of the fundamental tenets of the Law of Attraction. Our vibrational frequency is raised by positive emotions like love, joy, and gratitude, which eases the manifestation of our desires. On the other hand, negative feelings depress us and obstruct the flow of prosperity.

Tapping strengthens the Law of Attraction by helping us remove the negative emotions that prohibit us from staying in a high vibrating state. It is not enough to just repeat positive affirmations if there are underlying doubts or worries. We may negate those feelings by tapping, which will make us clear and open to manifestation.

Beginning with the basics of tapping and moving on to more complex methods for removing ingrained ideas, we will examine the concrete procedures for incorporating tapping into your manifestation practice in the upcoming chapters. Combining these techniques with the Law of Attraction will lead to a life that is more abundant, fulfilling, and powerful.

Step-by-Step Guide to Tapping

It is easy to learn and practise tapping. The precise points to tap on and the order to follow for best outcomes will be covered in this chapter. Energy blockages can be released by tapping on the various tapping points, which correspond to the body's meridians.

The basic tapping sequence includes the following points:

1. Karate chop point (side of the hand)
2. Eyebrow point
3. Side of the eye
4. Under the eye
5. Under the nose
6. Chin point
7. Collarbone point
8. Under the arm
9. Top of the head

By combining these physical points with a focus on the specific issue or belief you want to work on, you will activate the body's energy system and release trapped emotions.

What to Say While Tapping: Crafting Affirmations for Manifestation

The verbal part is a crucial part of tapping. You repeat statements that highlight the problem as you tap on the various spots. After recognising the issue *(e.g., "Even though I have this fear of failure...")*, the sentences usually conclude with a positive affirmation *(e.g., "I deeply and completely accept myself")*. This procedure releases the emotional burden attached to the problem while enabling the mind to face it.

We will go into detail in the upcoming chapters on how to customise your tapping practice to achieve aims, such as attracting success, fortune, health, or love. This guide will give you a complete toolkit to help you tap your way to the life you want.

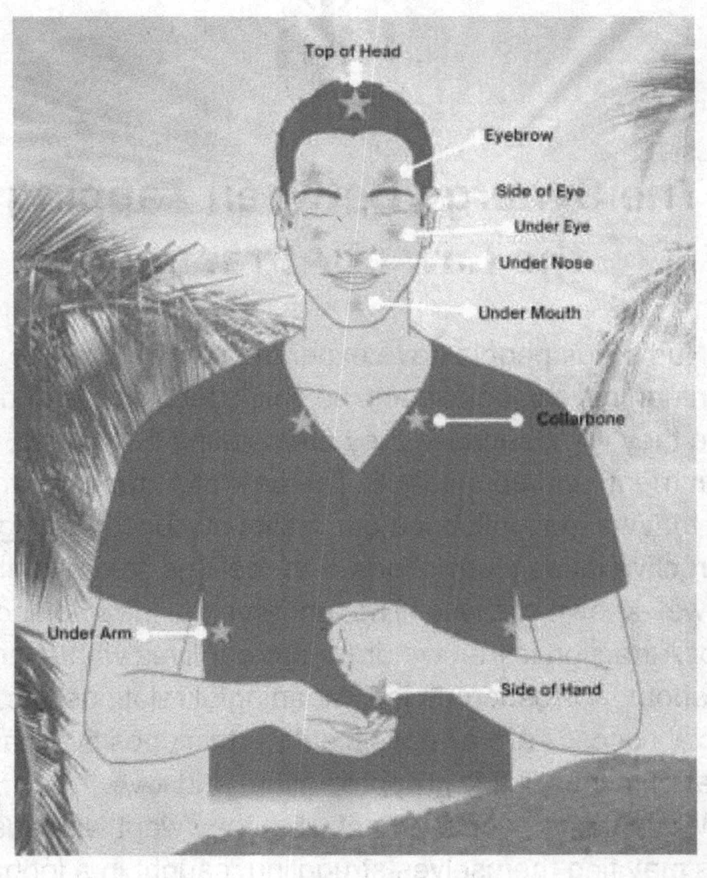

Chapter 1

The Synergy Between Tapping and the Law of Attraction

Numerous people have experimented with a wide range of spiritual, psychological, and scientific techniques to design the life they want because they are seeking happiness, contentment, and abundance. The Law of Attraction, which holds that we may influence our reality by concentrating on constructive ideas, convictions, and feelings, is one of the most well-known of these. The fundamental idea behind the Law of Attraction is that we draw into our lives whatever we think about. A prosperous job, meaningful relationships, and financial success are all possible if we think positively and cultivate feelings like joy, appreciation, and love.

While some people attract what they want with ease, others may find themselves struggling, caught in a loop of negative thinking, emotional blockages, and self-sabotaging beliefs. This is where tapping, also known as Emotional Freedom Technique (EFT), comes into perform. However, for many people who try to apply this principle, the process of manifesting their desires is not always as simple as they would like.

Tapping is a potent practice that focusses on unpleasant feelings, experiences, or limiting beliefs while gently tapping on acupressure points on the body. This straightforward technique helps to clear the path for the constructive flow of energy that is necessary for successful manifestation by releasing energetic blockages and re-establishing emotional equilibrium. Tapping can aid you in more fully aligning with the feelings and ideas needed to draw your desires when paired with the Law of Attraction.

How Tapping and the Law of Attraction Work Together

It is useful to first understand a fundamental manifestation principle—that emotions are energy—to completely understand how tapping strengthens the Law of Attraction. There is a frequency at which everything in the cosmos, including our thoughts and feelings, resonates. Positive emotions like joy, love, and thankfulness cause us to vibrate at a high frequency, which is in harmony with the energy of prosperity, prosperity, and well-being. On the other hand, our vibrational frequency decreases when we are mired in negative emotions like fear, irritation, or doubt, and we unintentionally draw more of the same negativity into our lives.

The Law of Attraction, which is based on the idea that like attracts like, is based on this vibrational basis. Therefore, we must elevate our frequency to match the vibration of what we wish to attract if we want to manifest the life we want. For this reason, a lot of Law of Attraction practitioners stress the value of affirmations, visualisation, and positive thinking. The problem is that unresolved emotional blocks can make it impossible to genuinely believe and experience such affirmations, regardless of how many times we repeat positive statements or how hard we try to concentrate on what we want.

At this point, tapping becomes a useful technique. Tapping neutralises the emotional charge associated with self-doubt, limiting beliefs, and prior traumas by allowing us to release the negative energy that keeps us back. We can lower the fight-or-flight reaction, relax the nervous system, and tell the brain that it is okay to let go of stress and anxiety by tapping on body locations. This not only lessens the severity of negative feelings but also makes space for more constructive ideas, sentiments, and convictions to become known.

The Benefits of Tapping for Manifestation

Thinking about what we wish is not enough for the manifestation process; we also need to feel as though we already have it. This is the most difficult aspect for many. When you are having financial difficulties, how do you feel abundant? After experiencing heartbreak, how do you feel about love? When you are overwhelmed by negative feelings, it can seem impossible to achieve the emotional alignment required by the Law of Attraction.

Tapping can help bridge that gap by:

- **Releasing Negative Emotions**: Emotions that reduce our vibratory frequency and prevent us from attracting what we want, such as fear, anger, irritation, and doubt, can be released through tapping.

- **Rewiring Negative Thought Patterns:** By reducing the stress reaction in the brain, tapping enables us to overcome negative thought patterns and form empowering new beliefs.

- **Creating Emotional Space for Positive Manifestation:** Once we remove the negative emotional charge around an issue, we create space for positive thoughts and feelings to take their place, allowing us to vibrate at the frequency of our wishes.

- **Improving Emotional Resilience:** It is simpler to keep alignment with the positive emotions needed for manifestation when tapping is used to lessen the emotional intensity of prior traumas, limiting beliefs, and anxieties.

By integrating tapping into your manifestation practice, you can break through emotional barriers and align more fully with the positive energy of what you want to attract. Tapping not only makes the Law of Attraction more accessible but also provides a practical tool for addressing the emotional obstacles that often stand in the way of successful manifestation.

A Practical Approach to Manifestation

Tapping provides a realistic, firsthand method of working with emotions and energy, even if the Law of Attraction is sometimes linked to mystical or metaphysical ideas. Anyone can master this technique, regardless of their manifestation experience or background. You will see a change in your emotional state as well as start to perceive observable changes in your external environment if you integrate tapping into your everyday routine.

We will go into detail on how to use tapping to improve your manifestation practice in the upcoming chapters. Before diving deeper into the science underlying tapping, we will first go over the fundamentals of the technique, including how it releases emotional blocks. Next, we will look at the Law of Attraction's tenets and how tapping strengthens this effective manifestation technique.

Additionally, you will learn how to tap on specific places and how to make affirmations that will help you achieve your goals. In addition to techniques for overcoming limiting beliefs and developing a regular tapping practice, we will go over tailored tapping routines for certain goals including success, love, prosperity, and health. Along the way, we will also share actual success stories of people who used tapping and the Law of Attraction to change their lives.

This book will give you the useful tools and insights you need to advance your manifestation practice, regardless of how long you have been using tapping and the Law of Attraction. By the end of this trip, you will know how to use the Law of Attraction to your fullest potential to create the life you genuinely want, in addition to knowing how to tap your way to emotional freedom.

The next chapter will take you through the fundamental principles of tapping, how it works with the body's energy system, and how to perform it effectively. Once you understand the basics of tapping, you will be ready to unlock its full potential as a tool for manifestation.

After discussing how tapping and the Law of Attraction work together, let us take a closer look at tapping itself. You will learn in detail how tapping functions, how it affects the body's energy flow, and why it is so successful in clearing emotional blockages in the upcoming chapter. Once you have mastered the fundamentals, you will be prepared to apply tapping to your own life and start more easily and clearly manifesting your wishes.

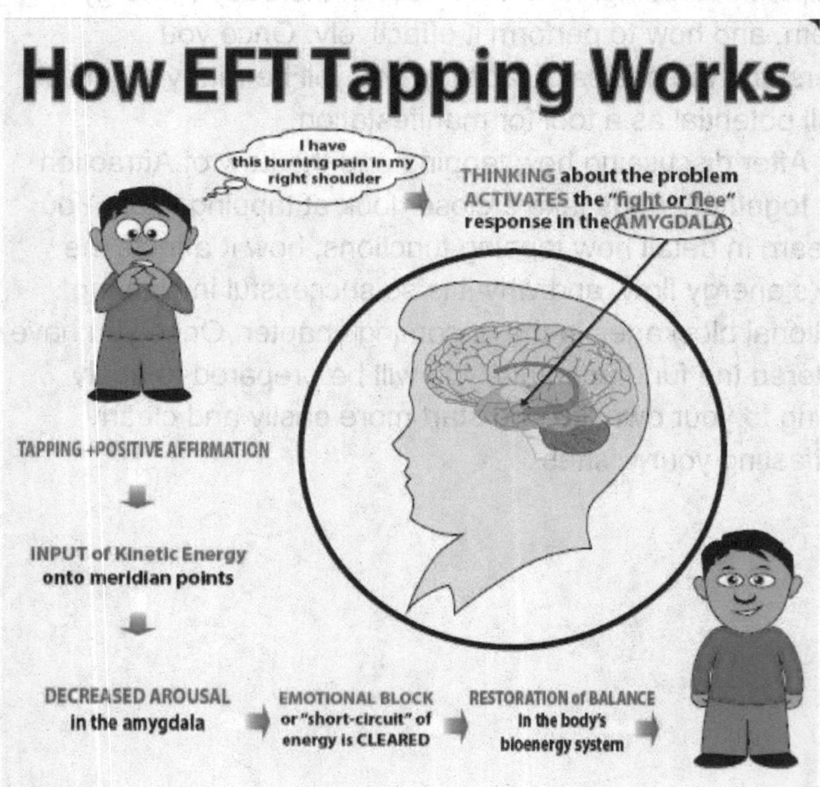
How EFT Tapping Works
I have this burning pain in my right shoulder
THINKING about the problem ACTIVATES the "fight or flee" response in the AMYGDALA
TAPPING +POSITIVE AFFIRMATION
INPUT of Kinetic Energy onto meridian points
DECREASED AROUSAL in the amygdala
EMOTIONAL BLOCK or "short-circuit" of energy is CLEARED
RESTORATION of BALANCE in the body's bioenergy system

Chapter 2

Understanding Tapping: The Basics and Energy Flow

The Emotional Freedom Technique (EFT), sometimes known as tapping, is a technique that blends aspects of contemporary psychology and traditional Chinese acupressure. EFT helps in releasing negative energy blockages and re-establishing equilibrium by gently tapping on areas of the body's meridian system while concentrating on emotional or physical problems. Tapping is a flexible technique for anyone wishing to strengthen their manifestation practice using the Law of Attraction and improve their emotional well-being because of its tremendous influence and ease of use.

Tapping could appear strange at first. How, after all, can talking about your feelings and touching on certain bodily parts produce such potent changes? We must examine two basic ideas to understand this: the body's energy flow and the impact of emotional blockages on manifestation.

What is Tapping?

The idea behind tapping is that the body has a complex energy system, sometimes known as the meridian system. This idea comes from Traditional Chinese Medicine, which holds that energy, or Qi, moves along particular bodily channels known as meridians. The body and mind run at their best when energy flows freely via these meridians, resulting in clarity, emotional balance, and good health. On the other hand, mental disruptions like anxiety, fear, or frustration as well as physical discomfort can result from blocked or sluggish energy.

Tapping entails focussing on a particular emotional or physical problem while stimulating important places along the meridians. In this way, tapping helps the discharge of energy blockages that are causing emotional distress. The bad feelings and restrictive ideas that keep us from achieving our goals are believed to be caused by these obstacles.

In a standard tapping session, you choose a specific problem to address, like stress, failure-related anxiety, or a money-related limiting belief. You can relieve the accompanying energy barrier by finding the unpleasant feeling or belief as you tap on the meridian points. Once the bad energy has been released, you may concentrate on introducing beliefs or affirmations that are in line with your manifestation goals.

Energy Flow in the Body: The Meridian System

Energy moving through the body is not a novel idea. Traditional medical practices like acupuncture, acupressure, and Ayurveda have been using the body's energy to heal and balance people for thousands of years. There are twelve main meridians that stand for various organs and bodily functions, according to traditional Chinese medicine. These meridians serve as conduits for energy, supporting and promoting mental and physical well-being.

Energy cannot flow smoothly when the meridians are blocked, which leads to imbalances. These imbalances might show up as physical symptoms like headaches, exhaustion, or chronic pain, but they are also often felt as negative emotions like anxiety, fear, despair, or rage. Tapping's function is to clear these obstructions so that energy can flow freely once more, and equilibrium is restored.

We can communicate with the brain and body that it is safe to relax and release the blocked energy by tapping on locations along the meridians. This significantly affects the nerve system, helping in stress reduction, mental calmness, and the modification of unfavourable emotional patterns. Tapping allows us to address the underlying causes of emotional distress instead of merely its symptoms when paired with a focus on thoughts or beliefs.

How Emotional Blockages Affect Manifestation

About the Law of Attraction, your feelings have a significant impact on what you draw into your life. As a type of energy, emotions vibrate at various frequencies, just like any other energy. The energy of your wishes is in harmony with the high frequency vibrations of positive emotions like love, joy, gratitude, and abundance. However, negative emotions that resonate at a lower frequency, such as fear, doubt, anger, and impatience, generate resistance throughout the manifestation process.

This resistance is often brought on by emotional obstacles that put us in a negative vibratory state, such as ingrained fears, beliefs, or traumas. For instance, a subconscious feeling that you are not deserving of prosperity can run as a blocker in your energy system if you wish to generate financial success. Your efforts to attract abundance will be undermined by the emotional energy surrounding that limiting idea, regardless of how hard you concentrate on it.

Tapping is a tool for releasing these emotional blockages. By tapping on the meridian points while acknowledging your negative emotions or limiting beliefs, you neutralise the emotional charge and allow the energy to flow more freely. Once the negative emotion is released, you can replace it with a positive affirmation or belief that supports your manifestation goals. This process helps to reprogram your subconscious mind, aligning your energy with the thoughts and feelings necessary for attracting your desires.

The Key Tapping Points

To cut any obstructions in the flow of energy, tapping is most effective on a few precise spots on the body that correspond to the meridians.

The basic tapping points used in EFT are as follows:

1. Karate Chop Point (side of the hand): Found on the outer edge of your hand (on the Pinky side), this is the point used at the beginning of the tapping sequence. It is often used when saying your set-up phrase, which acknowledges the issue on which you are tapping.

2. Eyebrow Point: This point is found at the start of your eyebrow, just above the bridge of the nose. It helps to release tension and negative emotions associated with the issue at hand.

3. Side of the Eye: Found on the bone at the outer corner of the eye, this point is often associated with fear and anxiety.

4. Under the Eye: Found directly below the eye on the cheekbone, this point helps to relieve fear and worry.

5. Under the Nose: Found just below the nose and above the upper lip, this point is linked to shame and guilt.

6. Chin Point: Found just below the lip, in the crease between the lower lip and the chin. Tapping here helps release feelings of embarrassment and insecurity.

7. Collarbone Point: This point is found just below the collarbone, where the collarbone meets the sternum. It is one of the most powerful tapping points and helps to release a wide range of emotions including anxiety, overwhelm, and indecision.

8. Under the Arm: Found about four inches below the armpit (in line with the nipple for men and on the bra line for women), this point is associated with stored emotions like anger, fear, and frustration.

9. Top of the Head: The decisive point is at the crown of your head. Tapping here helps to integrate the emotional release and create a sense of balance.

During the tapping process, these locations are used in a particular order. As you progress through each point, you softly tap on the points with your fingertips while concentrating on the problem at hand, which could be a bodily experience, limiting belief, or negative emotion. Focused attention and physical stimulation enable the brain to process and release the related emotions.

Why Tapping Works: The Mind-Body Connection

The mind-body connection is one of the reasons tapping works so well. Negative emotions are not merely mental feelings; they are also stored in the body as physical sensations and energy blockages. When we suffer from emotional pain or trauma, the body often stores these feelings, which can lead to tension, discomfort, or disease.

Both the cerebral and bodily levels are affected by tapping. Tapping helps the body relieve tension and trapped energy by physically stimulating the meridian points. At the same time, tapping enables the mind to process and release the negative thought patterns linked to that emotion by concentrating on that emotion or idea. Tapping is a particularly potent method for emotional healing and manifestation because of its dual approach, which works with the mind and body.

Numerous studies have proved how tapping can effectively reduce physical pain as well as tension and anxiety. The amygdala, the area of the brain in charge of the fight-or-flight response, has been shown to be less active after tapping. Tapping serves to lessen the body's physiological reaction to stress by soothing this area of the brain, which enables us to move from a state of dread to one that is more open and relaxed. This helps us transition from a state of resistance to one of accord with our desires, which is essential for manifestation.

The Emotional Freedom Tapping Process

You are prepared to start using tapping to remove your own emotional blockages now that you know the fundamentals and how it interacts with the body's energy system. We will go into more detail about the tapping procedure in the upcoming chapter, including how to use set-up statements, find difficulties to work on, and decide the proper tapping point sequence.

Learning the fundamentals of tapping will provide you an effective instrument for removing the restricting ideas and negative feelings that prevent you from moving forward. This fundamental knowledge will help you approach the Law of Attraction with more emotional clarity, enabling you to manifest your desires more easily and confidently, no matter whether you are new to tapping or have used it previously.

In the next chapter, we will walk through the tapping procedure in depth, providing you with a practical roadmap to start practicing EFT for emotional freedom and manifestation.

Chapter 3:

The Science Behind Tapping: Mind and Body Connection

Tapping, sometimes referred to as the Emotional Freedom Technique (EFT), may seem like a straightforward technique, but it has profoundly transformed effects on the body and mind. Although tapping has its origins in ancient energy medicine, new scientific studies are starting to confirm its neurological and psychological effects. Knowing the science underlying tapping helps explain why it is such an effective method for increasing the Law of Attraction, clearing emotional blocks, and lowering stress.

We must investigate the mind-body connection—the complex interrelationship between our emotional experiences, thought patterns, and physical health—to completely recognise the potential of tapping. This relationship is crucial to how we manage stress, how we create and hold onto beliefs, and eventually how we bring our dreams to life. Tapping helps to re-establish equilibrium in the mind and body by addressing the emotional and physiological reactions that arise when we face difficulties.

How Tapping Affects the Brain

The body and mind are the same. Our ideas and feelings have a direct impact on how the brain functions, which in turn affects our behaviour and physical well-being. The stress response, sometimes referred to as the fight-or-flight reaction, is triggered by unpleasant emotions like anxiety, fear, or rage. The amygdala, a little almond-shaped region in the brain that is essential for processing emotions, especially stress and fear, is mostly responsible for controlling this reaction.

The amygdala primes the body to respond to a perceived threat by causing the release of stress hormones such as cortisol and adrenaline. Although this reaction is essential for life in perilous circumstances, it can become overwhelming and even detrimental when brought on by common stressors like negative thoughts, unresolved trauma, or limiting beliefs. The fight-or-flight response can become chronically activated, which can result in increased anxiety, sadness, physical tension, and even disease.

By relaxing the amygdala, tapping lowers the body's physiological stress response. According to studies, tapping lowers cortisol levels, which are higher under stressful situations. Tapping allows the nervous system to go from a state of elevated stress to one of peace and balance by activating the body's meridian points while concentrating on unpleasant feelings or memories.

In addition to reducing stress at once, this relaxing impact aids in brain rewiring. Over time, tapping develops new neural pathways that support more empowered, positive ways of thinking by lessening the emotional intensity of negative thoughts and beliefs. Since tapping helps you change your perspective to match the feelings and ideas needed to bring your wishes to life, it is especially pertinent when used in conjunction with the Law of Attraction.

The Fight-or-Flight Response and Limiting Beliefs

Understanding the relationship between limiting beliefs and the brain's stress response is crucial to understanding why tapping is so successful for manifestation. Deeply rooted mental patterns known as limiting beliefs influence our feelings of both the outside world and us. These ideas, which have an impact on everything from our expectations of success to our sense of self-worth, are often developed throughout early childhood or after traumatic events.

When you try to manifest your desires, these limiting beliefs can cause fear or resistance because the brain interprets change as a threat and sets off the fight-or-flight response. For instance, if you were raised with the belief that money is scarce or that you are unworthy of love, these beliefs become ingrained in your subconscious mind. This can cause you to feel anxious, self-conscious, or frustrated when you try to attract what you want, even if you are using positive affirmations or visualisations.

By reducing the emotional intensity associated with limiting beliefs, tapping aids in breaking this pattern. You are telling your brain that it is okay to let go of an old pattern when you tap on meridian points while concentrating on a negative thought or feeling. To successfully manifest your desires, you must be able to move from fear to an emotional state that is in line with them.

Tapping and the Body's Energy System

Traditional Chinese Medicine, which has long acknowledged the significance of preserving a free flow of energy, or Qi, throughout the body, has set up a connection between tapping and the body's energy system. In this system, energy travels through meridians, which are pathways that carry energy to every part of the body; when energy flows freely, we experience physical and emotional health; when it becomes blocked or stagnant, we experience discomfort, illness, and emotional imbalances.

To relieve obstructions and restore the normal circulation of energy, tapping stimulates areas along these meridians. This allows tapping to promote physical healing in addition to relieving emotional anguish. Many people see significant changes after just a few tapping sessions because of this dual influence on the body and mental state.

The effect of tapping on the energy system is particularly noteworthy when considering the Law of Attraction. Emotions are energy, according to the Law of Attraction, and what we attract into our lives is decided by the energy we release. Our vibratory frequency is lowered by negative emotions like fear, uncertainty, or impatience, which makes it challenging to align with the higher frequencies of success, love, and abundance. Tapping helps raise your vibrational frequency by clearing these obstructions, which makes it easier to draw in the things you want.

The Role of the Prefrontal Cortex in Manifestation

Tapping has an impact on the prefrontal cortex, another critical area of the brain, in addition to soothing the amygdala. Higher-level cognitive processes including planning, reasoning, and decision-making are controlled by the prefrontal cortex. It is essential for keeping us concentrated on our goals and aiding us in making wise decisions that suit our preferences.

When the fight-or-flight response is engaged, the prefrontal cortex becomes less active. This makes it tougher to think clearly, focus on answers, or feel motivated to take constructive action. Rather, worry, anxiety, and survival instincts take over the brain, causing procrastination, self-defeating behaviour, and a general feeling of being "stuck."

Tapping helps the prefrontal brain work better by lowering stress and relaxing the amygdala. This implies that you are more likely to feel motivated, clear-headed, and goal-focused after tapping. Your brain is more capable of helping you make choices and conduct actions that are consistent with your manifestation goals.

Research and Evidence Supporting Tapping

Even though tapping may have started out as an alternative therapy, there is mounting scientific evidence that it works. Tapping has been shown in many studies to dramatically lower stress, anxiety, melancholy, and even physical pain.

Some of the most notable research includes:

- **Cortisol Reduction**: According to a study by **Dr. Dawson Church**, after just one tapping session, participants' levels of the stress hormone cortisol dropped by 24%. This research lends credence to the notion that tapping promotes emotional equilibrium and relaxation by reducing the body's stress reaction.

- **PTSD and Trauma**: Tapping can be extremely helpful in treating PTSD, according to several studies. One study found that after six tapping sessions, PTSD symptoms in veterans were reduced by 63%. This shows that tapping can lessen the emotional intensity of past traumas, which is important for overcoming limiting beliefs and attracting positive outcomes.

- **Emotional Wellbeing**: Apart from its effects on stress and trauma, studies have also proved that tapping enhances mental health in general. After employing tapping to treat their emotional problems, participants in several studies have reported feeling more empowered, cheerful, and self-assured.

According to the research, tapping can help induce long-lasting emotional changes that promote constructive transformation in addition to lowering stress and anxiety. By cutting the emotional and energy obstacles that stand in your way, these changes, when paired with the Law of Attraction, can be extremely helpful in aiding you in realising your goals.

Tapping, Neuroplasticity, and Rewiring Thought Patterns

The potential of tapping to promote neuroplasticity—the brain's ability to create new neural connections and reorganise itself in response to novel experiences—is among its most intriguing features. In the brain, each of our thoughts, feelings, and beliefs forms a neural pathway. A concept or feeling gets stronger the more times we repeat it. It becomes challenging to alter long-standing thought habits as these pathways become firmly set up over time.

However, tapping lessens the emotional intensity of negative ideas and beliefs, which helps to break these old patterns. This enables the brain to develop new, more powerful neural pathways that promote manifestation and positive thinking. You may start rewiring your brain to focus on what you want to attract instead of what you mistrust or fear by tapping on a regular basis. This can eventually result in significant mental shifts and an increased ability to bring your goals to life.

How Tapping Prepares the Mind for Manifestation

Tapping produces the ideal mental and emotional condition for manifestation through lowering stress, relaxing the nerve system, and rewiring thought patterns. It aids you in shifting from a resistance state, where uncertainty and fear rule your life, to an alignment state, where you feel clear, assured, and in control of drawing in the things you want.

You are creating the ideal environment for your manifestation practice to thrive when you combine tapping with the Law of Attraction. You can start concentrating more intently on your aims, visualisations, and affirmations after you are free of the emotional obstacles and limiting ideas that have prevented you from moving forward. Tapping produces a potent synergy between your mind, body, and the energy of your desires in addition to aiding in the removal of negative energy.

We are going to investigate the Law of Attraction's principles and examine how our ideas and feelings influence our reality in the upcoming chapter. To fully use these approaches and include tapping into your manifestation practice, you must understand these ideas. You will have the skills and information necessary to manifest the life you genuinely want and tap your way to emotional liberation by the end of this trip.

Chapter 4

The Law of Attraction Explained

Spiritual searchers, self-help enthusiasts, and even scientists who want to learn more about the power of thought and emotion have all been enthralled with the Law of Attraction. This idea is straightforward but profound: you attract into your life what you think and feel. The energy you release through your thoughts, feelings, and beliefs is continuously affecting the reality you perceive whether you are aware of it or not. The Law of Attraction, when properly understood and used, may be a potent instrument for bringing about your goals, be they greater prosperity, satisfying relationships, improved health, or personal development.

The fundamental ideas of the Law of Attraction, its operation, and the reasons why feelings and beliefs are so important in deciding our reality will all be covered in this chapter. Gaining an understanding of these ideas will lay the groundwork for utilising tapping to improve your manifestation technique. You will have a better grasp of how your thoughts and feelings shape your experiences and how to intentionally match them with your desires by the end of this chapter.

The Core Principles of the Law of Attraction

The principle that like attracts like lies at the core of the Law of Attraction. This implies that you will receive a reflection of your ideas, feelings, and beliefs in the form of experiences from the energy you project into the universe. You are more likely to get favourable results if you continuously concentrate on feeling and thinking positively. On the other hand, you will draw more of the same into your life if you focus on negative ideas or emotions of inadequacy.

There are three key principles that underpin the Law of Attraction:

1. Everything is Energy

According to modern physics, especially quantum physics, energy makes up everything in the cosmos. This encompasses both material and intangible items, such as ideas and feelings. Every idea and feeling you have had a unique vibrational frequency that interacts with the environment. Understanding that you are continuously releasing a vibrational frequency that draws events and circumstances of a similar frequency is the foundation of the Law of Attraction. For this reason, if you wish to attract positive results, it is crucial to nurture happy thoughts and feelings.

2. The Power of Focus

The Law of Attraction functions based on the concentration principle. What you concentrate on grows. You are unintentionally drawing more of those undesirable experiences into your life if you spend most of your time thinking about things you do not want, such as loneliness, bad health, or financial difficulties. Problems become clearer in your reality the more you concentrate on them. But when you start concentrating on what you do desire, like love, prosperity, or success, you start drawing those things into your life. Everything you continuously focus on will expand in your reality because your mind is like a magnet.

3. Emotions are the Key to Manifestation

Emotions are the real force behind the Law of Attraction, even though thoughts are crucial to the manifestation process. This is since emotions have a vibrational frequency that is far higher than that of thoughts alone. Even if you intentionally consider what you want to happen, you will find it difficult to draw it into your life if your feelings are not in line with it. For instance, your ability to attract wealth will be hampered if you are trying to manifest financial plenty but are afraid or nervous about money. When you feel affluent, on the other hand, even before you reach your financial aims, you align yourself with the vibration of abundance, which eases the attraction of wealth into your life.

The key to successful manifestation lies in emotional alignment. It is not enough to just think about what you want—you must also feel as though you already have it. This is where tapping becomes an invaluable tool. By using tapping to release negative emotions and beliefs that are out of alignment with your desires, you can more easily cultivate the positive emotions that are essential for manifestation.

How the Law of Attraction Works: The Thought-Emotion Cycle

The fact that the Law of Attraction functions within the thought-emotion cycle is among its most crucial concepts. Depending on how you control your thoughts and emotions, this cycle can either work in your favour or against you.

Here is how the thought-emotion cycle works:

1. Thoughts Generate Emotions: You experience an emotional reaction to every thought you have. For instance, depending on your expectations for the outcome, you can feel nervous or thrilled about an impending presentation at work. Your thoughts generate feelings that are in line with the ideas you are thinking about. While negative ideas tend to produce feelings like fear, wrath, and uncertainty, positive thoughts typically produce feelings like joy, confidence, and hope.

2. Emotions Influence Your Actions: Your behaviours are then influenced by the feelings you experience. You are more likely to take audacious, aggressive actions to reach your aim if you are enthusiastic and confident about the possibility. On the other side, you can pause, put things off, or not carry out anything at all if you are nervous or unsure. Your emotions serve as the motivation for your actions.

3. Actions Shape Your Reality: The world you experience is shaped by the things you do or do not do. Positive outcomes are likely to materialise if your activities are in line with your desires. You will find it difficult to get the results you want, though, if your emotions cause you to act (or not act) in ways that are inconsistent with your aims.

4. Reality Reinforces Your Thoughts: Your first ideas are then supported by the outcomes you meet in your reality. A positive feedback loop will be created if you take constructive action and experience success. This will boost your confidence and motivation even further. On the other hand, you risk reinforcing negative thoughts and feelings about yourself or your talents if your activities result in failure or dissatisfaction.

To support your desires, the Law of Attraction helps you in escaping negative cycles and transitioning into a constructive thought-emotion-action loop. You can end the self-defeating cycle and set up new, empowering thinking patterns that support your aims by practicing tapping to release unpleasant emotions and limiting beliefs.

The Role of the Subconscious Mind

Your subconscious mind shapes your life much more than you may think, even though you may consciously concentrate on your desires. Your innermost expectations, worries, and beliefs are stored in your subconscious mind; many of these were developed during formative years or important life events. Like an internal blueprint, these subconscious ideas affect how you see the world and react to possibilities.

For instance, even if you consciously want to succeed, your actions and emotions will be influenced by your subconscious attitude that you are not deserving of it. You can start to mistrust your skills, feel unmotivated, or sabotage opportunities. The subconscious mind can help or hurt your ability to bring your desires to life in this way.

The subconscious mind is not fixed, which is excellent news. Through emotional intensity and repetition, it can be reprogrammed. This is the point at which tapping and the Law of Attraction work their magic. You can start reprogramming your subconscious mind with new, empowered thoughts that support your manifestation goals by employing tapping to eliminate the emotional charge surrounding restrictive beliefs.

Why Most People Struggle with the Law of Attraction

Despite its clear simplicity, many individuals find it difficult to implement the Law of Attraction in their daily lives. This is often the result of their emphasis on optimistic thinking at the expense of the underlying feelings and ideas that are impeding their attempts for manifestation. Common obstacles include:

1. Unresolved Emotional Blockages: Fear, humiliation, guilt, and anger are just a few of the unresolved emotions that many people hold from their prior experiences. They are unable to completely align with their desires because of the energetic blocks created by these emotions. These unresolved feelings may run as a roadblock to manifestation, even if you intentionally concentrate on what you want.

2. Limiting Beliefs: Long-standing mental patterns known as limiting beliefs control your feeling of the world and of yourself. Since these ideas often function subconsciously, it might be challenging to detect their effects. Thoughts like "I am not good enough," "I do not deserve happiness," or "Success is hard to achieve" are examples of common limiting beliefs. These ideas prevent you from attracting the things you want by acting as imperceptible obstacles.

3. Emotional Misalignment: Emotional misalignment is one of the main obstacles people meet while utilising the Law of Attraction. Even if you have a conscious desire, it will be difficult for you to manifest if your emotions are not in line with it. For instance, your manifestation efforts will be thwarted if you feel unworthy of love or fear rejection, even though you may wish to attract a loving connection.

4. Inconsistent Focus: According to the Law of Attraction, you must constantly concentrate on the things you wish to draw in. But a lot of people go between concentrating on their desires and obsessing about their uncertainties or anxieties. Because of the conflicting signals this inconsistency produces, it is more difficult to draw in favourable results.

Because of these challenges, manifestation may seem elusive and frustrating. However, you can deal with these issues at their core by integrating tapping with the Law of Attraction. By removing the emotional obstacles and limiting ideas that impede your manifestation efforts, tapping enables you to stay emotionally aligned with your aspirations and keep constant attention.

The Importance of Emotional Alignment

Emotions are essential to successful manifestation, as we have explored. Thinking about what you want is not enough; you also need to feel as though you already have it. The most critical part of successfully applying the Law of Attraction is emotional alignment.

You vibrate at the same frequency as the results you wish to attract when you are emotionally in line with your aspirations. This shows that your beliefs, feelings, and thoughts are all in line with your aims. Being emotionally aligned helps taking creative action, keeping motivation, and drawing in chances that support your goals.

Achieving emotional alignment in the face of uncertainties, concerns, or limiting beliefs is, of course, a challenge. This is the point at which tapping becomes quite useful. Positive emotions like joy, confidence, and appreciation can take root when you use tapping to cut negative emotions and limiting beliefs. Attracting the results you want will be lot simpler if you are in an emotional alignment condition.

Conclusion

Though it takes more than just optimistic thinking, the Law of Attraction is a potent tool for building the life you want. It requires a clear, goal-oriented mindset and emotional connection with your desires. A useful and efficient method for getting rid of the mental and emotional barriers preventing you from completely embracing the Law of Attraction is tapping. You can fully use the Law of Attraction and start bringing your desires to life more easily and confidently by letting go of negative emotions, clearing your mind, and retraining limiting beliefs.

We will examine how tapping strengthens the Law of Attraction and how to use it as a tool to speed up your manifestation practice in the upcoming chapter. We will examine the emotional liberation tapping offers and how it makes room for manifestation to thrive. You will discover how to employ tapping to unlock your full manifestation potential through real-world examples and detailed instructions.

Chapter 5

How Tapping Enhances the Law of Attraction

At its core, the Law of Attraction depends on your ability to align your thoughts, emotions, and energy with the outcomes you want. Although many people only concentrate on positive thinking, emotional alignment—the feeling that your desires have already materialized—is the key to true manifestation. However, achieving this emotional alignment can be difficult, particularly when you are being held back by subconscious blocks, limiting beliefs, or past traumas. In these situations, tapping can be a transformative tool.

By helping you in releasing the negative emotions and energy barriers that keep you from supporting a high vibrating state, tapping, also known as Emotional Freedom Technique (EFT), complements the Law of Attraction. Tapping, when done properly, can help you get rid of the emotional clutter that prevents your desires from manifesting and make room for them to grow.

This chapter will examine how tapping strengthens the Law of Attraction, emphasising how it releases limiting beliefs, promotes emotional freedom, and helps you become more in line with your goals. Additionally, you will discover how to incorporate tapping into your manifestation practice to enhance the outcomes and have more success drawing in the things you want.

The Power of Emotional Freedom

Since your vibrational frequency is influenced by the emotions you carry, it is crucial for effective manifestation. For example, if you are trying to manifest abundance but are stressed, anxious, or afraid of money, these negative emotions will create a vibrational block that prevents you from aligning with the energy of wealth. Similarly, if you are seeking a loving relationship but carry feelings of unworthiness or fear of rejection, those emotions will disrupt your ability to attract love. This is one of the biggest advantages of tapping: it creates a sense of emotional freedom, which allows you to let go of limiting beliefs and negative emotions that are holding you back.

You can release yourself from this emotional baggage by tapping. You can relax the brain's stress reaction and discharge the energetic charge associated with unpleasant emotions by tapping on acupressure points while paying attention to your feelings. By neutralising negative emotions like fear, doubt, and frustration, this approach helps you become more open and emotionally clear. You may more readily align with the good emotions—such as joy, appreciation, and confidence—that are essential for manifestation when you are emotionally liberated.

Clearing Emotional Blocks to Manifestation

Emotional blocks, which can be rooted in past experiences, limiting beliefs, or deep-seated fears that we may not even be consciously aware of, create resistance that makes it difficult to support a high vibration and focus on your goals. This is why many people struggle to manifest their desires because they are unaware of the emotional blocks that are undermining their efforts.

For instance, you can unknowingly hold the belief that money is hard to get by or that you are not worthy of wealth if you have previously struggled financially. These ideas cause you to feel anxious and afraid about money, which lowers your vibrational frequency and prevents you from drawing in wealth. Similarly, you might have an unconscious conviction that love causes suffering if you have been harmed in earlier relationships. This idea can keep you from really embracing new romantic opportunities.

One useful technique for finding and removing these emotional obstacles is tapping. You can release the energetic charge that keeps you trapped in earlier patterns by tapping on the meridian points and bringing the negative emotion or belief to the surface. This helps you go forward with more ease and confidence by rewiring the brain's response to the problem and relieving emotional strain.

How Emotional Blocks Impact the Law of Attraction

You attract what you feel, according to the Law of Attraction. You will produce energy resistance even if you have a conscious desire if your emotions are not in line with that desire. This is the reason a lot of individuals have trouble manifesting their aims; they concentrate on what they want but are either scared, frustrated, or unsure of their ability to get it.

The emotional obstacle that prevents manifestation can be removed by tapping. You can overcome the fear, uncertainty, and annoyance that keep you from really embracing the energy of your aspirations by tapping on your emotional barriers. By removing these emotional obstacles, you make room for manifestation and make it easier for your wishes to come to you.

Reprogramming Limiting Beliefs

Tapping is quite efficient at aiding you in reprogramming limiting beliefs, which are the subconscious ideas that influence your feeling of the world and yourself, in addition to releasing unpleasant emotions. Limiting beliefs affect everything from your sense of self-worth to your expectations of success, and they are often formed during early infancy or because of major life events.

For example, you may hold limiting beliefs such as:
- ✓ *"I am not worthy of love."*
- ✓ *"Money is the root of all evil."*
- ✓ *"Success is only for other people, not me."*
- ✓ *"I'm not smart or capable enough to achieve my goals."*

Even if you are making a conscious effort to concentrate on positive results, these beliefs serve as imperceptible obstacles that prevent you from achieving your goals. Limiting beliefs are effective because they function subconsciously, so you might not even be aware of how much they are affecting your feelings and actions.

Tapping works by addressing both the emotional and cognitive elements of limiting beliefs. When you tap on a belief, you acknowledge the emotional force behind it, which helps you remove the negative energy associated with that belief. Tapping also gives you the opportunity to incorporate new, empowering beliefs that support your manifestation aims. You can start rewiring your brain to support your desires by tapping while repeating positive affirmations.

For instance, if you are working on manifesting financial abundance, you could tap on the belief ***"Even though I've always struggled with money, I deeply and completely accept myself."*** As you continue tapping, you can introduce a new belief, such as "I am open to receiving abundance in all forms" or ***"I deserve to live a life of financial freedom."*** Over time, this process helps to shift your subconscious beliefs from a state of lack to one of abundance.

Creating Space for Positive Emotions

A critical aspect of the Law of Attraction is the ability to feel as though your desires have already been fulfilled. This sentimental alignment is what raises your vibrational frequency and allows you to attract beneficial outcomes. However, it can be difficult to cultivate positive emotions if you are weighed down by negative feelings or not resolved emotions.

By removing the negative energy that is connected to fear, doubt, or frustration, tapping eases the experience of positive emotions like joy, gratitude, and love. Following the removal of these emotional barriers, you can concentrate on the positive emotions that are in line with your desires.

For instance, tapping can aid in relieving anxiety related to the chance of failure while you are trying to materialise a new job. You can more readily concentrate on feeling assured and enthusiastic about your career prospects once the fear has subsided. Your vibrational frequency rises because of this emotional change, increasing your chances of drawing in the employment prospects you want.

How to Use Tapping in Your Manifestation Practice

It is easy to incorporate tapping into your manifestation practice, and it works wonders. You can improve your ability to manifest your desires by routinely using tapping to release emotional blocks, rewire limiting beliefs, and foster good emotions.

Here is how to get started:

1. Find Your Limiting Beliefs or Negative Emotions

Finding the limiting beliefs or emotional barriers that are preventing you from manifesting is the first step in using tapping. Fear, uncertainty, frustration, or certain ideas like *"I am not good enough"* or *"I do not deserve success"* could be examples of these. Be truthful with yourself about the feelings and ideas that are causing you to meet resistance in your life.

2. Create a Set-Up Statement

After deciding the emotion or belief you wish to address, make a set-up statement that affirms self-acceptance and acknowledges the problem. You might use the following as your set-up statement if you are experiencing financial anxiety: ***"Even though I feel anxious about my finances, I deeply and completely accept myself."***

3. Tap Through the Sequence

Tap on the meridian points in the proper order while you repeat your set-up phrase, starting with the karate chop point and working your way through the eyebrow, side of the eye, under the eye, etc. Focussing on the bad feeling or thought you wish to let go of, keep tapping.

4. Introduce a Positive Affirmation

Introduce a positive affirmation that supports your manifestation aims after tapping on the negative feeling or idea. Saying ***"I am open to receiving financial abundance"*** or ***"I trust that money flows to me easily"*** are two examples of how to address financial worry. Repeat your affirmation while tapping through the process one again.

5. Repeat as Needed

Consistent tapping practice yields the best results. You may need to perform the practice many times to totally remove deeply set up emotions or ideas. You will eventually notice that the issue's emotional energy lessens and that your thoughts and feelings are more in line with positive ones.

The Synergy of Tapping and the Law of Attraction

Tapping's real power is found in its capacity to remove the mental and emotional barriers that stand in the way of your complete acceptance of the Law of Attraction. Combining a manifestation practice with tapping produces a synergy that enhances your outcomes. While the Law of Attraction aids you in concentrating on the good feelings and ideas that correspond with your wishes, tapping enables you to let go of negative emotions and limiting beliefs that decrease your vibrational frequency.

You can reach a condition of emotional alignment with your aims by combining the two strategies, which will make it simpler to draw in the results you want. Tapping can aid you in removing the emotional obstacles that have been preventing you from achieving your goals of success, love, health, and financial wealth. This will allow you to live a life that is fuller of possibilities and fulfilment.

Conclusion

By offering a useful and efficient way to overcome mental and emotional resistance, tapping strengthens the Law of Attraction. It supports your manifestation goals by aiding you in letting go of negative emotions, reprogramming limiting beliefs, and making room for happy emotions. You can become more emotionally liberated, connect with the energy of your desires, and create the life you really want by incorporating tapping into your everyday routine.

A detailed tutorial on tapping will be covered in the upcoming chapter, along with information on the precise tapping places, how to formulate strong setup statements, and how to organise your tapping session for best effects. Gaining ability in the fundamentals of tapping will provide you with a strong instrument to aid in your manifestation process.

Chapter 6

Step-by-Step Guide to Tapping

Anyone may learn tapping, sometimes referred to as Emotional Freedom Technique (EFT), which is a straightforward but effective technique. You can promote emotional clarity and cut energy blockages by tapping on certain acupressure points while concentrating on a specific problem or emotion. We will walk you through the entire tapping process in this chapter, including which points to tap, how to construct powerful set-up statements, and how to organise your tapping sequences to improve your manifestation practice.

You may release negative emotions, dispel limiting beliefs, and promote emotional alignment with your manifestation goals by learning the fundamentals of tapping. This book will help you improve your tapping technique and use it more successfully in your everyday life, regardless of your level of experience.

Tapping Points: The Basics

Getting acquainted with the main tapping spots on the body is the first step in studying EFT. The meridians, which are channels that transport energy throughout the body, line up with these places. You can clear any blockages that might be creating emotional or physical discomfort and encourage energy flow by tapping on these places.

Here is a list of the basic tapping points and their locations:

1.**Karate Chop Point**:
The tapping sequence starts with this point, which is on the outside of the hand (the fleshy part on the side of the hand, beneath the little finger). Additionally, this is where you say your setup statement.

2.**Eyebrow Point**:
This location is found close to the nose bridge at the inner edge of the eyebrow. Emotions such as fear and frustration can be released by tapping here.

3.**Side of the Eye**:
Found on the bone at the outer corner of the eye, this point helps to address emotions related to fear and anger.

4.**Under the Eye**:
Directly below the eye on the cheekbone, this point is associated with fear and anxiety, and tapping here can help relieve these feelings.

5. **Under the Nose**:
Found between the nose and upper lip, this point can help address feelings of shame, embarrassment, or guilt.

6. **Chin Point**:
Found in the crease between the lower lip and chin, tapping here can help release self-doubt and insecurity.

7. **Collarbone Point**:
The collarbone point is found just below the collarbone, near where it meets the sternum. It is one of the most powerful tapping points and can help release anxiety, overwhelm, and indecision.

8. **Under the Arm**:
This point is found about four inches below the armpit (in line with the nipple for men or on the bra line for women). It is used to release feelings of insecurity, anger, and fear.

9. **Top of the Head**:
The decisive point is at the crown of the head. Tapping here helps to integrate the emotional release and create a sense of balance and calm.

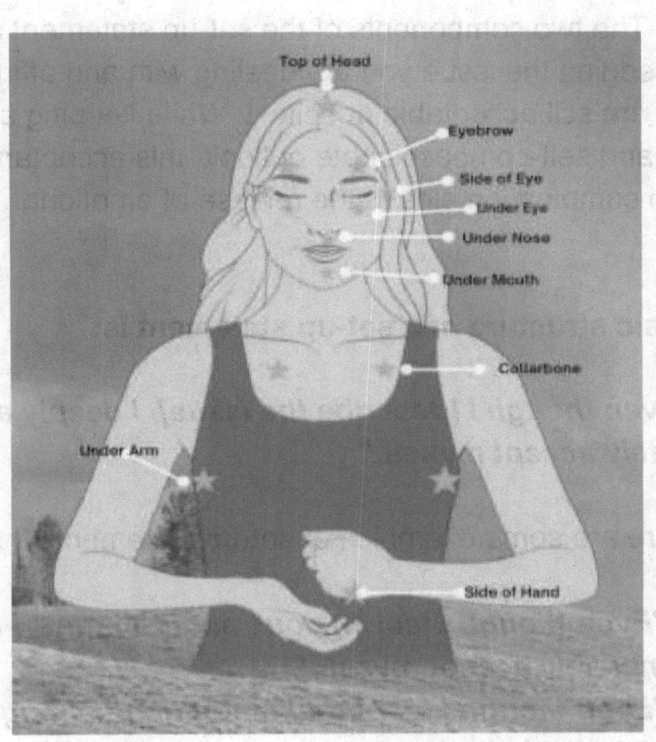

When you get familiar with the tapping points, the EFT sequence becomes intuitive and simple to practise. These tapping points are the basis of the EFT sequence and tapping on each one in order while concentrating on your issue helps to clear emotional and energetic blocks.

Creating an Effective Set-Up Statement

It is crucial to draft a set-up statement that precisely says the problem you wish to address before you start tapping. The two components of the set-up statement are acknowledging the issue you are dealing with and affirming that you are still acceptable despite it. While keeping a positive and self-compassionate outlook, this acceptance and attention combination aids in the release of emotional barriers.

The basic structure of a set-up statement is:

"Even though I [describe the issue], I deeply and completely accept myself."

Here are some examples of set-up statements that you can use:

- *"Even though I feel anxious about money, I deeply and completely accept myself."*
- *"Even though I fear that I'm not good enough to succeed, I deeply and completely accept myself."*
- *"Even though I feel frustrated about not reaching my goals, I deeply and completely accept myself."*
- *"Even though I have a fear of failure, I deeply and completely accept myself."*

Affirming your self-acceptance creates a safe space for the emotion or belief to be released, which makes tapping more effective. This is important because emotional healing starts with acceptance, and by acknowledging the negative emotion or belief in the set-up statement, you bring it into your awareness without resisting it.

The Tapping Sequence: A Step-by-Step Guide

Once you have created your set-up statement, you are ready to begin the tapping sequence. Follow these steps for a complete round of tapping:

1.Start with the Set-Up Statement

Begin by tapping on the karate chop point on the side of your hand. As you tap, repeat your set-up statement aloud three times. For example, ***"Even though I feel anxious about money, I deeply and completely accept myself."***

2.Move Through the Tapping Points

After completing the set-up statement, start tapping through the other points in the following order. As you tap on each point, repeat a short phrase that summarises the issue on which you are working.

For example, if your issue is anxiety about money, you could say, ***"This anxiety about money"*** at each point.

1. **Eyebrow Point**: *"This anxiety about money."*
2. **Side of the Eye**: *"This anxiety about money."*
3. **Under the Eye**: *"This anxiety about money."*
4. **Under the Nose**: *"This anxiety about money."*
5. **Chin Point**: *"This anxiety about money."*
6. **Collarbone Point**: *"This anxiety about money."*
7. **Under the Arm**: *"This anxiety about money."*
8. **Top of the Head**: *"This anxiety about money."*

As you repeat the phrase, tap on each spot five to seven times. You can tap with any hand, and tapping on either side of the body is OK. It is okay to be too strict with the tapping procedure; it should feel comfortable and natural.

3. Complete Multiple Rounds

Take a deep breath and assess your feelings after finishing a thorough tapping session. Has the emotion or belief changed in intensity? On a scale of **0 to 10**, you can show how intense the feeling is, with ten being the strongest emotion. Repeat the tapping pattern until the emotion seems less intense if it is still high.

4. Introduce a Positive Affirmation

Once you feel the negative emotion or belief has been reduced, you can introduce a positive affirmation that aligns with your desired outcome. For example, if you were tapping on anxiety about money, you could now introduce an affirmation like, ***"I trust that abundance flows to me easily"*** or ***"I am open to receiving financial prosperity."***

As you tap through the points once again, repeat the affirmation. This aids in solidifying the new conviction and setting up it in your subconscious.

5. End with a Final Round

Tap through the points one more time to finish the process, paying attention to any tension or emotional residue that may still be present. This last round aids in ensuring that the issue's emotional burden has been completely removed.

How to Use Tapping for Specific Manifestation Goals

Now that you know the fundamentals of tapping, you may start using it to achieve manifestation goals. Tapping can help you in bringing your feelings and beliefs into line with your goals, whether they be to attract wealth, a fulfilling relationship, better health, or professional success.

Here is how to tailor tapping to different goals:

For Financial Abundance:

If you are manifesting more money or financial freedom, start by finding any negative emotions or beliefs you have about money. These could include fear of not having enough, guilt about wanting wealth, or a belief that money is hard to come by.

Create a set-up statement that acknowledges the issue, such as, ***"Even though I feel anxious about my financial situation, I deeply and completely accept myself."*** As you tap through the points, focus on releasing the fear and anxiety around money.

Once the intensity of the negative emotions decreases, introduce a positive affirmation like, ***"I am open to receiving financial abundance"*** or ***"I trust that money flows to me easily and effortlessly."*** Repeat the positive affirmation while tapping through the points again to reinforce the new belief.

This process helps to shift your focus from fear and scarcity to one of abundance and trust, allowing you to align your energy with the vibration of financial prosperity.

For Manifesting Love:

Address any thoughts of inadequacy, rejection anxiety, or broken hearts that might be impeding your ability to attract love if you want to attract a loving relationship. ***"Even though I'm afraid I won't find love, I deeply and completely accept myself"*** may be your set-up statement.

Release any emotional blocks related to love by tapping through the sequence while concentrating on these feelings and anxieties. Introduce affirmations like ***"I am worthy of love"*** or "I am open to receiving a loving and fulfilling relationship" once you feel lighter. To attract the love and connection you want; this helps you raise your emotional frequency.

For Career Success:

Find any limiting thoughts or feelings you may have about your skills, self-worth, or fear of failing if your aim is to create professional success. For instance, you can worry about your employment prospects or believe ***that "I am not good enough to succeed."*** Some examples of set-up statements ***include "Even though I fear I'm not good enough for success, I deeply and completely accept myself."***

Let go of any fear, self-doubt, or frustration you may be holding as you tap through the pattern. Then, use affirmations that are uplifting, such as ***"I am capable of achieving great success"*** or ***"I attract opportunities that align with my highest potential."*** This makes it easier for you to create career advancement by bringing your energy into alignment with ambition and confidence.

For Improved Health:

When trying to manifest improved health, concentrate on any limiting ideas, disappointments, or anxieties you may have about your well-being. This could include thinking that keeping health is hard, feeling frustrated by disease, or fearing that one will not recover. One way to set up the scene might be to say, ***"Even though I'm frustrated with my health, I deeply and completely accept myself."***

Let go of the feelings associated with your health issues while you tap. After these feelings have subsided, start using affirmations such ***as "My body is healthy, vibrant, and strong" or "I trust in my body's ability to heal."*** This enables you to align your body and mind with healing energy and change your focus to a state of health and wellbeing.

Structuring a Daily Tapping Routine

The secret to tapping for manifestation is consistency. Tapping can be a regular exercise that helps you stay emotionally in line with your aims if you integrate it into your daily schedule. The ideal way to set up a daily tapping routine is as follows:

1. Morning Tapping for Setting Intentions

Tapping into your intents and aspirations is a wonderful way to start the day. You can tap on any negative feelings or beliefs that may have come up during the night or when you wake up during this quick five-to-ten-minute session. Set a positive tone for the day and use this time to overcome any opposition. For instance, if you are worried about money in the morning, tap briefly to calm yourself down. Then, make a financial abundance intention by saying, ***"I am open to receiving wealth and prosperity today."***

2. Tapping During the Day

Throughout the day, be mindful of your thoughts and feelings. Spend a few minutes tapping if you sense any doubt, frustration, or anxiety beginning to sneak in. To let go of the unpleasant emotion, this could be as easy as tapping through the points for a few minutes. You may stop these feelings from intensifying and impeding your manifestation tries by dealing with them at once.

3. Evening Tapping for Reflection and Release

Spend some time thinking back on your feelings and ideas at the end of the day. Did you experience any unpleasant feelings or limiting beliefs during the day? Take advantage of this moment to tap for a longer period with the goal of removing any last resistance. You could tap through the points and let go of the day's emotional baggage during this ten-to-fifteen-minute exercise.

Positive affirmations that support your goals, like ***"I am in alignment with the energy of my desires"*** or ***"I trust that everything is working out in my favour,"*** can be used to wrap up your session.

4. Tapping Before Visualisation or Meditation

Tapping can also be used as a pre-visualization or pre-meditation technique. By quickly tapping out any negative emotions, you can create a focused and calm mental state that enhances the effectiveness of visualisation or meditation. After tapping out any resistance, you can visualise your goals with more clarity and emotional alignment.

How Long Should You Tap?

One of the best things about tapping is that it may be completed in a few minutes, or more if you are dealing with a particularly challenging problem. In general, setting intentions for the day or removing little emotional obstacles can be carried out in a quick 5- to 10-minute session. However, you might wish to tap for 15 to 20 minutes if you are working through a more profound emotional problem or limiting belief.

The key is to listen to your body and emotions. After each round of tapping, check in with yourself to see if the intensity of the emotion has decreased. If it has, you can introduce a positive affirmation and close the session. If the intensity is still high, continue tapping until you feel a sense of emotional relief.

How to Measure Your Progress

It is useful to rate the intensity of the emotion or belief before and after each tapping session to decide how successful they are. This is called the *Subjective Units of Distress Scale (SUDS)*, and it asks you to rate how strongly you feel on a scale of 0 to 10, where 0 is neutral and ten is the most acute.

Take a moment to rate the intensity of the emotion or belief before you start tapping. For instance, you might give the intensity an eight out of ten if you are tapping into financial worry. Check in with yourself and reevaluate the intensity after each tapping session. You should see a decrease in intensity as the session goes on. This is a useful method for checking your development and deciding whether you have overcome sufficient emotional resistance.

Using Tapping for Long-Term Manifestation Success

Tapping is a tool that can help you succeed with the Law of Attraction and reach long-term emotional freedom; it is not just a temporary solution. You can set up a mental and emotional environment that eases your manifestation goals by regularly employing tapping to cut negative emotions and limiting beliefs. Your power to manifest your desires will grow over time, and you will discover that it gets simpler to keep a pleasant, high-vibration condition.

Keep in mind that manifestation is a process rather than a quick fix. By removing the emotional obstacles in your path, tapping aids you in becoming more in line with your aims; yet it is crucial to have patience and have faith in the process. Tapping turns becomes a potent tool for changing your perspective, elevating your vibration, and building the life you really want as you continue to use it in your daily life.

Conclusion

You may improve your manifestation practice with tapping, which is a very flexible and powerful instrument. EFT can be used to rewire limiting beliefs and remove emotional resistance by learning the fundamentals of the tapping sequence, crafting set-up statements, and adding positive affirmations. You may make the emotional space necessary to fully connect with your desires and make the Law of Attraction more successful in your life by tapping daily.

In the upcoming chapter, we will concentrate on creating effective set-up statements and affirmations that you may use when tapping to hasten the manifestation process. To make your manifestation practice as successful as possible, you will discover how to customise your affirmations to your unique aims and develop a stronger emotional bond with your wishes.

Chapter 7

What to Say While Tapping: Crafting Affirmations for Manifestation

Knowing what to say when tapping is one of the most crucial parts of the method. As important as the actual tapping is, so are the phrases you use when tapping. You can make a potent weapon that not only helps you let go of bad feelings but also helps you stay focused on the things you want to manifest by creating powerful affirmations and set-up statements. When paired with tapping, words' energy can improve your emotional alignment with your desires.

In this chapter, we will study how to build set-up statements, develop powerful affirmations, and organise your words during tapping sessions to produce the best results. Whether you are new to tapping or looking to develop your practice, learning what to say during your sessions will allow you to grasp the full power of this technique.

The Role of Language in Tapping

The words you choose to use when tapping to create your desires aid focus your attention. By bringing the problem to light, they enable you to completely recognise and deal with any negative feelings or limiting ideas that might be impeding your attempts at manifestation. Additionally, the language you use when tapping helps to change your energy and thinking towards a state of emotional alignment by reinforcing good thoughts and aims.

There are two main stages of language use in tapping:

1. Set-Up Statements: These affirmations affirm self-acceptance while acknowledging the negative emotion, belief, or problem on which you are working. This procedure eases healing by reducing the emotional intensity of the problem.

2. Affirmations: Affirmations aid in introducing new, constructive beliefs that support your aims after dealing with the negative emotion. These affirmations strengthen the feelings and ideas needed for manifestation while also raising your vibrational frequency.

A balanced tapping session requires both affirmations and set-up statements. While affirmations aid you in aligning with the energy of what you want to attract, setup statements aid in the release of emotional obstacles.

Creating Effective Set-Up Statements

Each tapping session starts with the set-up statement, which affirms self-acceptance and acknowledges the problem you are trying to solve. This combination of self-compassion and honesty is essential because it creates a safe space for the negative emotion to be released while enabling you to face it without passing judgement.

A set-up statement typically follows this format:

Even though I [describe the issue], I deeply and completely accept myself."

For example:
Even though I feel anxious about money, I deeply and completely accept myself."
Even though I'm afraid I won't find love, I deeply and completely accept myself."
Even though I doubt my ability to succeed, I deeply and completely accept myself."

You allow yourself to release the unpleasant emotion when you accept the problem without opposition. Affirming self-acceptance also helps you avoid being too obsessed with the issue, which can cause more emotional strain. The set-up statement, on the other hand, gently brings the problem to the surface for resolution.

Tips for Creating Set-Up Statements

- **Be Specific:** The set-up statement will work better if you describe the problem in more detail. For instance, rather than saying, ***"Even though I feel stressed,"*** try to find the cause of the stress: ***"Even though I feel anxious about not*** *having enough money"* or *"Even though I feel stressed about my workload."*

- Acknowledge Both the Emotion and the Belief: Sometimes, your issue may involve both a strong emotion and an underlying belief. For example, *"Even though I feel anxious about not making enough money, and I believe I'm not capable of earning more, I deeply and completely accept myself."*

- Affirm Self-Acceptance: The key part of the set-up statement is the affirmation of self-acceptance. This ensures that, despite the problem, you keep a sense of self-worth and compassion. Variations of this affirmation could include *"I love and accept myself"* or *"I deeply respect myself."*

Crafting Powerful Affirmations for Manifestation

Once you have completed a round of tapping using your set-up statement, it is time to introduce positive affirmations that align with your manifestation goals. Affirmations help to shift your focus from the problem to the solution, replacing negative beliefs with empowering thoughts.

An effective affirmation is:

- Present-focused: The affirmation should be said in the present tense, as if your desire has already been fulfilled. This creates emotional alignment with the outcome you want to attract. For example, instead of saying *"I will be wealthy,"* say *"I am open to receiving abundance"* or *"I am financially secure."*

- Positive: Affirmations should focus on what you want, not on what you are trying to avoid. For instance, instead of saying *"I am not stressed,"* say *"I am calm and relaxed."*

- Emotionally Charged: The more emotion you can bring into your affirmation, the more powerful it becomes. Feel the emotion of already having what you want as you repeat the affirmation. For example, *"I am deeply grateful for the financial abundance that flows to me"* carries a strong emotional resonance.

Here are some examples of affirmations for different manifestation goals:

Financial Abundance:
- ✓ *"I am open to receiving financial abundance."*
- ✓ *"Money flows to me easily and effortlessly."*
- ✓ *"I am grateful for the wealth and opportunities in my life."*

Love and Relationships:
- ✓ *"I am worthy of a loving and fulfilling relationship."*
- ✓ *"I attract love and joy into my life effortlessly."*
- ✓ *"I am open to giving and receiving love freely."*

Career Success:
- ✓ *"I am capable of achieving great success in my career."*
- ✓ *"I attract opportunities that align with my highest potential."*
- ✓ *"I am confident and motivated to succeed."*

Health and Wellbeing:
- ✓ *"My body is healthy, strong, and full of energy."*
- ✓ *"I trust in my body's ability to heal and thrive."*
- ✓ *"I am grateful for my vibrant health and wellbeing."*

Using Affirmations During Tapping

Start a new tapping session with your positive affirmation after finishing a round that was centred on your set-up statement. Repeat the statement aloud as you tap through each point, giving yourself permission to really engage with the emotion it expresses. ***"I am open to receiving wealth"*** is one way to tap through each point if your goal is financial abundance.

As if the affirmation were already true, experience it. Imagine yourself living the reality you are confirming, and then let your feelings soar to the level of that result's energy. Using the Law of Attraction to bring your desires to life requires this emotional harmony.

Here is a step-by-step example of using an affirmation during tapping:

1. **Eyebrow Point:** *"I am open to receiving wealth."*
2. **Side of the Eye**: *"I am grateful for the abundance in my life."*
3. **Under the Eye:** *"Money flows to me easily and effortlessly."*
4. **Under the Nose:** *"I am worthy of financial freedom."*
5. **Chin Point:** *"I am aligned with the energy of abundance."*
6. **Collarbone Point**: *"I trust that money comes to me in expected and unexpected ways."*

7. Under the Arm: *"I am financially secure and prosperous."*
8. Top of the Head: *"I attract wealth and opportunity into my life every day."*

Tailoring Affirmations to Your Specific Goals

It is crucial to customise affirmations to your own aims to make them effective. Decide the result you wish to achieve first, then consider your feelings if it were already a reality. Create your affirmation based on those feelings.

For example:
- If you are manifesting a new job, think about how you would feel once you have been offered the position: confident, excited, motivated. Your affirmation could be, ***"I am confident and excited about my new career opportunity."***
- If you are manifesting better health, consider how you would feel if you were already healthy: vibrant, energised, grateful. Your affirmation might be, ***"I am grateful for my body's health and strength."***
The more personal and emotionally charged your affirmation is, the more effective it will be in helping you align with your desires.

Combining Visualisation with Affirmations

Combine visualisation with affirmations and tapping for an even more potent manifestation technique. Take a moment to close your eyes and see yourself living the reality you are affirming while you repeat your affirmations. Imagine yourself living the prosperous life, the devoted relationship, the rewarding job, or the vibrant health you have always desired. Give yourself permission to experience the feelings that come with already having what you want.

This combination of tapping, affirmations, and visualisation creates a strong energetic signal that aligns you with your desired outcome. By tapping to release resistance, affirming your desires, and visualising your success, you amplify the power of the Law of Attraction.

Common Mistakes to Avoid When Crafting Affirmations

While affirmations are a powerful tool, they can lose effectiveness if not crafted correctly. Here are some common mistakes to avoid:

- **Using Future Tense:** Affirmations should always be said in the present tense, as though the outcome is already true. Avoid phrases like ***"I will"*** or ***"One day I'll have..."*** Instead, say ***"I am"*** or ***"I have."***

- **Focusing on Lack**: Make sure your affirmations focus on what you want to attract, not on what you lack. For example, instead of saying "I don't want to be in debt," say "I am financially secure and free of debt."

-**Lack of Emotion:** Making sure you completely connect with the emotion underlying the affirmation is crucial since just repeating words without feeling will not have much of an effect.

- **Inconsistent Practice:** To rewire your thoughts and emotions, you must repeat affirmations repeatedly over time.

For the best effects, combine tapping with affirmations every day, but do not expect improvements right away.

Conclusion

A key part of successfully using EFT for manifestation is knowing what to say when tapping. You may build a strong process that not only releases bad emotions but also connects you with the energy of your desires by creating detailed and well-thought-out set-up statements and then following them up with emotionally charged affirmations.

We will look at tapping for aims, including success, love, riches, and health, in the upcoming chapter. Using the power of affirmations, you will discover how to design personalised tapping routines for each of these areas, enabling you to confidently and clearly manifest your own desires.

Chapter 8

Tapping for Specific Goals:
Health, Wealth, Love, and Success

Tapping is an incredibly versatile tool that can be applied to a wide range of goals. Whether you are aiming to improve your health, attract financial abundance, manifest a loving relationship, or conduct career success, tapping can help you remove the emotional blocks standing in the way of your desires. By combining tapping with specific positive affirmations tailored to each goal, you can align your thoughts and emotions with the outcomes you wish to manifest.

In this chapter, we will explore how to use tapping for health, wealth, love, and success. You will learn how to structure your tapping sessions for each of these areas, using carefully crafted set-up statements and affirmations that are designed to help you overcome limiting beliefs and emotional resistance. By the end of this chapter, you will have a clear framework for using tapping to achieve your specific manifestation goals.

Tapping for Health

One of the most crucial pillars of a happy existence is good health. However, a lot of people suffer from long-term medical conditions, psychological stress, or self-limiting ideas about their body's ability for recovery. These obstacles may hinder your physical recovery and keep you from feeling well and energetic. By releasing the emotional tension, anxiety, or annoyance linked to health problems, tapping can help your body regain equilibrium and well-being.

Common Emotional Blocks to Health

- Fear of illness or disease.
- Frustration with chronic health conditions.
- Limiting beliefs about the body's ability to heal.
- Emotional stress contributing to physical symptoms.

Example Set-Up Statements for Health

- ✓ *Even though I'm frustrated with my health, I deeply and completely accept myself."*
- ✓ *Even though I fear that my body won't heal, I deeply and completely accept myself."*
- ✓ *Even though I feel stressed and overwhelmed by my health issues, I deeply and completely accept myself."*

Example Affirmations for Health
- ✓ *My body is strong, healthy, and full of energy."*

✓ *I trust in my body's natural ability to heal and restore balance."*

✓ *I am grateful for my vibrant health and wellbeing."*

Step-by-Step Tapping for Health

1. Start with the Set-Up Statement: Start by repeating your set-up sentence while tapping on the karate chop spot. For instance, ***"Even though I'm frustrated with my health, I deeply and completely accept myself."*** While tapping, repeat this statement three times.

2. Tap Through the Points: As you tap through the other points (eyebrow, side of the eye, under the eye, etc.), repeat a short phrase that captures the emotion on which you are working. For example, ***"This frustration with my health"*** or ***"This fear about my body."***

3. Introduce Positive Affirmations: Once you feel the emotional charge decrease, introduce positive affirmations like, ***"My body is strong and capable of healing"*** or ***"I am grateful for my health."*** Tap through the sequence again, focusing on these positive affirmations.

4. Visualise Your Desired Outcome: Imagine that you are in excellent health while you tap. Imagine yourself feeling powerful, energised, and alive. By combining visualisation, affirmations, and tapping, you can strengthen your body's innate healing ability.

Tapping for Wealth

Financial abundance is a common goal for many people, but it can often be blocked by deep-seated fears, anxieties, or limiting beliefs around money. These beliefs, such as "Money is hard to come by" or "I don't deserve wealth," create resistance that prevents financial flow. Tapping can help you release these emotional blocks, shifting your energy from scarcity to abundance.

Common Emotional Blocks to Wealth

- Fear of not having enough money.
- Guilt or shame around wanting wealth.
- Beliefs that wealth is only for others, or that you do not deserve.
- Anxiety about financial stability.

Example Set-Up Statements for Wealth
- ✓ *"Even though I feel anxious about my financial situation, I deeply and completely accept myself."*
- ✓ *"Even though I don't believe I'm worthy of financial success, I deeply and completely accept myself."*
- ✓ *"Even though I fear I'll never have enough money, I deeply and completely accept myself."*

Example Affirmations for Wealth
- ✓ *"I am open to receiving financial abundance."*
- ✓ *"Money flows to me easily and effortlessly."*
- ✓ *"I deserve wealth, and I am grateful for the abundance in my life."*

Step-by-Step Tapping for Wealth

1. Start with the Set-Up Statement: Begin by tapping on the karate chop point while saying, ***"Even though I feel anxious about money, I deeply and completely accept myself."*** Repeat three times.

2. Tap Through the Points: As you tap through the points, repeat a phrase that reflects your emotional block, such as ***"This anxiety about money"*** or ***"This fear that I'll never have enough."***

3. Introduce Positive Affirmations: Once you have reduced the emotional intensity, introduce affirmations like, ***"I am open to receiving wealth"*** or ***"Money flows to me easily."*** Tap through the sequence again while focusing on these positive affirmations.

4. Visualise Abundance: As you tap, visualise yourself living in financial abundance. See yourself having more than enough money to meet your needs and desires. Feel the emotional relief of financial freedom.

Tapping for Love

Attracting love into your life can be challenging if you are carrying emotional wounds from past relationships or harbouring fears about rejection and vulnerability. These emotional blocks can prevent you from opening to love, even if you deeply want a relationship. Tapping helps you release these fears and align with the energy of love, making it easier to attract a healthy, fulfilling relationship.

Common Emotional Blocks to Love

- Fear of rejection or abandonment.
- Feelings of unworthiness or self-doubt.
- Pain from past relationships or heartbreak.
- Belief that love is hard to find or that you are not deserving of it.

Example Set-Up Statements for Love

✓ *"Even though I'm afraid I'll never find love, I deeply and completely accept myself."*

✓ *"Even though I feel unworthy of love, I deeply and completely accept myself."*

✓ *"Even though I'm afraid of getting hurt again, I deeply and "completely accept myself."*

Example Affirmations for Love

✓ *"I am worthy of love and connection."*

✓ *"I am open to giving and receiving love freely."*

✓ *"I attract loving and supportive relationships into my life."*

Step-by-Step Tapping for Love

1. Start with the Set-Up Statement: Begin by tapping on the karate chop point while repeating, **"Even though I'm afraid I won't find love, I deeply and completely accept myself."** Repeat three times.

2. Tap Through the Points: As you tap through the sequence, say a phrase like ***"This fear of not finding love"*** or ***"This feeling of unworthiness."***

3. Introduce Positive Affirmations: After reducing the emotional intensity, introduce affirmations like, ***"I am open to love"*** or ***"I am worthy of a fulfilling relationship."*** Tap through the sequence while repeating these affirmations.

4. Visualise Love and Connection: Imagine yourself in a caring, encouraging relationship as you tap. Imagine being content and in a relationship with someone who genuinely loves and appreciates you. Experience the happiness and tranquilly that come from being in a good relationship.

Tapping for Success

Whether you are aiming for personal or professional success, limiting beliefs such as ***"I'm not good enough"*** or ***"Success is hard to achieve"*** can hold you back from reaching your full potential. Tapping can help you overcome these internal barriers, build self-confidence, and align with the energy of success.

Common Emotional Blocks to Success

- Fear of failure or success.
- Doubts about your abilities or worthiness.
- Procrastination or lack of motivation.
- Belief that success is difficult to achieve or not meant for you.

Example Set-Up Statements for Success
- ✓ *"Even though I doubt my ability to succeed, I deeply and "completely accept myself."*
- ✓ *"Even though I'm afraid of failing, I deeply and completely accept myself."*
- ✓ *"Even though I procrastinate and avoid taking action, I deeply and completely accept myself."*

Example Affirmations for Success
- ✓ *"I am capable of achieving great success."*
- ✓ *"I attract opportunities that align with my highest potential."*
- ✓ *"I am confident, motivated, and ready to succeed."*

Step-by-Step Tapping for Success

1. Start with the Set-Up Statement: Begin by tapping on the karate chop point while saying, ***"Even though I doubt my ability to succeed, I deeply and completely accept myself."*** Repeat three times.

2. Tap Through the Points: Tap through the points while repeating a phrase like ***"This doubt about my success"*** or ***"This fear of failing."***

3. Introduce Positive Affirmations: Once the emotional intensity has decreased, introduce affirmations like, ***"I am confident and capable"*** or ***"I attract success with ease."*** Tap through the sequence while focusing on these affirmations.

4. Visualise Success: As you tap, visualise yourself achieving your goals. See yourself succeeding in your career, personal projects, or any area of life that is important to you.

Feel the excitement, pride, and satisfaction that come with achieving success.

Customising Your Tapping Practice

The important thing about tapping is that it can be customised to fit your own circumstances and aims. Whether it is success, love, wealth, or health, spend some time finding the beliefs or emotional blocks that are preventing you from moving forward in each area. Then, create affirmations and set-up statements that speak to your experience.

You may also find it helpful to journal about your goals and any emotional resistance you are experiencing. This can give you deeper insight into the root causes of your emotional blocks, making your tapping sessions more focused and effective.

Conclusion

Tapping is a highly flexible and effective technique that may be applied to any area of life. Whether you are aiming to better your health, attract financial prosperity, find love, or achieve success, tapping helps you erase emotional and mental barriers, allowing space for your dreams to manifest. You can tailor your tapping practice to meet your own aims by utilising set-up statements and affirmations.

The use of tapping to overcome limiting beliefs and rewire the subconscious mind for success will be discussed in the upcoming chapter. You will discover how tapping can aid you in overcoming deeply rooted thinking patterns that are impeding your ability to achieve your goals and how to swap them out for empowering ideas that will help you achieve them.

Chapter 9

Overcoming Limiting Beliefs: Using Tapping to Reprogram the Mind

Limiting beliefs are one of the most major hurdles to success in every aspect of life, whether it is health, prosperity, love, or career progress. These deeply set up ideas affect our feelings of ourselves and the world around us, often holding us back from realising our full potential. Even when we are actively working to achieve our goals, limiting beliefs keep us from progressing because they function as unseen barriers. The good news is that you can use tapping to recognise, question, and eventually dispel these beliefs, enabling you to set up new, empowered thought patterns that help you achieve your aims.

This chapter will cover the formation of limiting beliefs, how they affect your ability to materialise, and—most importantly—how to successfully rewire your subconscious mind through tapping. You can totally align with the energy of

your aspirations and break free from the mental and emotional limitations that have been impeding your growth by learning how to let go of limiting beliefs.

What Are Limiting Beliefs?

Subconscious ideas known as "limiting beliefs" limit your potential and have a detrimental impact on your emotions and behaviour. These ideas are often set up in childhood or because of challenging life events, and they are after strengthened by ingrained emotional and cognitive habits. Limiting beliefs might be hard to spot since they are often subtle and ingrained in your subconscious. Although they usually work in the background, they can have a significant impact.

Some common examples of limiting beliefs include:

- ✓ *I'm not good enough."*
- ✓ *I don't deserve success."*
- ✓ *Money is hard to come by."*
- ✓ *I'm not attractive enough to find love."*
- ✓ *Success is for other people, not me."*
- ✓ *I'll never be able to change my circumstances."*

These ideas can be a result of social conditioning, prior experiences, or even familial relationships, but they all have one thing in common: they make it harder to reach your aims and restrict your capacity to attract what you really want.

How Limiting Beliefs Impact Manifestation

The Law of Attraction runs on the notion that like attracts like. Your thoughts and emotions produce an electromagnetic frequency that attracts events that match that frequency. You attract favourable experiences and results when your ideas and feelings are in harmony with abundance, positivity, and self-worth. On the other hand, limiting beliefs cause a gap between your goals and your feeling of your own abilities.

For example, if you want to manifest financial abundance but subconsciously believe that *"Money is the root of all evil"* or *"I'm not good with money,"* these beliefs will block your ability to attract wealth, no matter how much you try to focus on abundance. Similarly, if you are seeking a fulfilling relationship but believe that *"I'm not worthy of love"* or *"Relationships always end in heartbreak,"* you may struggle to attract or sustain meaningful connections.

Energetic resistance is produced by limiting beliefs. They make it harder for you to connect with the energy of your aspirations by lowering your vibrational frequency and keeping you mired in ingrained emotional patterns. Tapping provides a useful method for dispelling these ideas, rewiring your brain, and refocusing your energy to get the results you want.

How Tapping Works to Reprogram the Subconscious Mind

Tapping works on two levels to help reprogram your mind and release limiting beliefs:

1. Emotional Release: Strong emotions like dread, frustration, worry, or shame are often present when someone has limiting beliefs. These feelings strengthen the belief and give it an emotional power that makes it more difficult to let go. You can remove the emotional charge attached to the limiting belief by tapping on the meridian points while concentrating on it. This will soothe the body's stress response and lessen the belief's influence over you.

2. Cognitive Reframing: As you release the emotional charge around a limiting belief, tapping allows you to introduce new, empowering beliefs. This process of cognitive reframing helps you create new neural pathways in the brain that support positive thinking. Over time, with consistent tapping, you can reprogram your subconscious mind to adopt beliefs that align with your goals and desires.

Finding Your Limiting Beliefs

Finding the precise beliefs that are holding you back is the first step in using tapping to overcome limiting beliefs. This can be difficult because limiting beliefs often function on a subconscious level, so you might not be completely aware of them, but there are a few techniques you can employ to bring these beliefs to the surface:

1. Notice Patterns of Self-Sabotage: Do you find yourself consistently falling short of your goals, despite your best efforts? Do you start projects only to abandon them halfway through, or find excuses not to act? Self-sabotage is often a sign of underlying limiting beliefs. For example, if you continually procrastinate on tasks related to your career, you may have a belief like ***"I'm not smart enough to succeed"*** or ***"I don't deserve success."***

2. Pay Attention to Negative Self-Talk: The way you talk to yourself, especially during moments of stress or frustration, can reveal a lot about your limiting beliefs. If you often find yourself saying things like ***"I'll never be able to do this"*** or ***"I always mess things up,"*** these statements can point to a deeper belief that is limiting your progress.

3. Reflect on Past Experiences: Limiting beliefs are often rooted in past experiences, particularly childhood or significant life events. Reflect on moments when you felt rejected, criticised, or unsupported. What conclusions did you draw about yourself in those moments? For example, if you were often told that you were not good enough, you may have internalised the belief that ***"I'm not capable."***

4. Examine Your Reactions to Success: How do you feel when you experience success or when someone compliments your abilities? If you feel uncomfortable, dismiss compliments, or downplay your achievements, this may show a limiting belief like ***"I don't deserve success"*** or ***"I'm not worthy of recognition."***

Once you have found your limiting beliefs, you can begin to use tapping to release them and replace them with empowering beliefs that support your manifestation goals.

Using Tapping to Release Limiting Beliefs

Here is a step-by-step guide to using tapping for releasing limiting beliefs:

1. Start with the Set-Up Statement:

Once you have found a limiting belief, create a set-up statement which acknowledges the belief and affirms self-acceptance. For example, if your limiting belief is ***"I'm not good enough to succeed,"*** your set-up statement could be, ***"Even though I believe I'm not good enough to succeed, I deeply and completely accept myself."***

Tap on the karate chop point while repeating the set-up statement three times.

2. Tap Through the Points:

As you tap through the other points, repeat a reminder phrase that reflects the limiting belief. For example, you might say, ***"This belief that I'm not good enough"*** or ***"This feeling of not being capable."***

- **Eyebrow point:**   *"This belief that I'm not good enough."*
- **Side of the eye:**   *"This belief that I'm not good enough."*
- **Under the eye:**   *"This feeling of being inadequate."*
- **Under the nose:**   *"This belief that I can't succeed."*
- **Chin point:**   *"This belief that I'm not capable."*
- **Collarbone point:**   *"This feeling of not being worthy."*
- **Under the arm:**   *"This belief that success is not for me."*
- **Top of the head:**   *"This belief that I'm not good enough."*

3. Repeat as Needed:

After each tapping session, check in with yourself to decide if the belief's emotional intensity has lessened. To rate the intensity on a scale of 0 to 10, use the Subjective Units of Distress Scale (SUDS). Continue tapping until the belief feels less emotionally charged if the intensity is still high.

4. Introduce a Positive Reframe:

Once the emotional intensity around the limiting belief has decreased, introduce a positive affirmation that replaces the old belief. For example, ***"I am capable of achieving success"*** or ***"I trust in my abilities and deserve to succeed."***

Tap through the sequence again while repeating the positive affirmation. This process helps to rewire your subconscious mind, replacing the old limiting belief with a new, empowering one.

5. Visualise Your Success:

As you tap, visualise yourself living the reality of the new belief. If your affirmation is ***"I am capable of achieving success,"*** see yourself confidently pursuing your goals, achieving success, and feeling proud of your accomplishments. This reinforces the new belief and helps align your energy with the outcome you want.

Examples of Limiting Beliefs and Tapping Set-Ups

Here are a few examples of common limiting beliefs and how to structure your tapping sessions to overcome them:

1. Limiting Belief: *"I don't deserve financial abundance."*

Set-Up Statement: ***"Even though I believe I don't deserve financial abundance; I deeply and completely accept myself."***

Affirmation: ***"I am worthy of financial success, and I am open to receiving abundance."***

2. Limiting Belief: *"Love always leads to heartbreak."*

Set-Up Statement: ***"Even though I believe love always leads to heartbreak, I deeply and completely accept myself."***

Affirmation: ***"I am open to receiving and giving love, and I trust that I deserve a fulfilling relationship."***

3. Limiting Belief: *"I'm not smart enough to succeed in my career."*

Set-Up Statement: ***"Even though I believe I'm not smart enough to succeed, I deeply and completely accept myself."***

Affirmation: ***"I am intelligent, capable, and confident in my abilities."***

Reinforcing New Beliefs Over Time

Tapping is a fantastic way to release limiting beliefs, but reprogramming your mind for success requires consistency. To ensure that your new beliefs become deeply ingrained and replace the old patterns that held you back, it is crucial to repeat the process on a regular basis.

You can reinforce your new beliefs by:
- **Tapping daily**: Incorporate tapping into your daily routine, focusing on different limiting beliefs or challenges as they arise. Over time, you will notice that your mindset shifts, and your new beliefs become second nature.

- **Journaling**: Keep a journal of your progress, writing down your new beliefs and how you feel about them. Journaling helps solidify these beliefs in your conscious and subconscious mind.

- **Visualising your success:** After each tapping session, take a moment to visualise yourself living in alignment with your new beliefs. See yourself experiencing the success, love, health, or abundance that these new beliefs make possible.

Conclusion

One of the most frequent barriers to manifestation is limiting beliefs, but you do not have to let them keep you back indefinitely. You can break free from old patterns and make room for new possibilities by reprogramming your subconscious mind and releasing the emotional charge associated with these beliefs through tapping. By removing the mental and emotional obstacles that prevent you from achieving your goals, tapping enables you to completely align with the life you wish to design.

We will look at how to create a tapping regimen that promotes long-term success and personal development in the upcoming chapter. To stay on course as you materialise your goals, you will discover how to create a regular practice that keeps you emotionally clear, focused, and in line with your aspirations.

Chapter 10

Daily Tapping Routine: Building a Consistent Practice

Manifestation is a continuous process that needs constant alignment of energy, thoughts, and emotions. Developing a regular tapping routine is one of the finest strategies to make sure you remain in line with your aspirations. You may rewire your mind for success, dissolve emotional obstacles, and lower stress by regularly practicing the Emotional Freedom Technique (EFT).

This chapter will walk you through the process of creating a tapping schedule that will help you on your path to manifestation. Tapping for a few minutes every day will help you overcome emotional resistance and improve your connection to your desires, which will make it simpler to attract what you look for.

Why a Daily Tapping Routine is Essential

Just as your body benefits from daily physical exercise, your mind and emotions receive help from consistent tapping practice. Emotional blocks, limiting beliefs, and stress can accumulate over time, even if you do not always notice them. A daily tapping routine helps you stay emotionally clear, centred, and focused on your goals.

Here are some key reasons why a daily tapping routine is essential for manifestation:

1. Emotional Maintenance: You might meet tense circumstances, anxieties, or uncertainties during the day, which could lead to emotional resistance. By releasing these emotional accumulations through a regular tapping program, you can keep them from solidifying into beliefs that impede your manifestation attempts.

2. Consistent Alignment: Manifestation requires that you keep alignment with your desires. Tapping daily ensures that you stay emotionally aligned with the outcomes you want to attract. By consistently clearing negative emotions, you keep your vibration high and focused on positivity.

3. Reinforcing New Beliefs: Reprogramming your subconscious thinking for success takes time and effort. A daily tapping program allows you to regularly reinforce the new, empowered ideas that support your aims. Old restricting patterns are gradually replaced by these ideas because of this process.

4. Boosting Emotional Resilience: There will inevitably be difficulties because life can be unpredictable. By developing emotional resilience, a daily tapping exercise helps you deal with setbacks and challenges without losing your cool. Maintaining your commitment to your manifestation journey requires this resilience.

How to Structure Your Daily Tapping Routine

A daily tapping routine does not have to be complicated or time-consuming. Even just 10-15 minutes a day can make a significant difference in how you feel emotionally and mentally. The key is to be consistent and intentional with your practice.

Here is a step-by-step guide to building a simple and effective daily tapping routine:

A. Morning Tapping: Setting Intentions for the Day

Start your day with a quick tapping practice that focusses on removing any emotional residue from the previous day and creating positive thoughts. Setting the tone for the rest of your day, morning tapping aids you in starting the day with attention, clarity, and a positive outlook.

Steps for Morning Tapping:

1. Find an Emotion or Goal: Begin by finding how you are feeling as you wake up. Do you feel anxious about the day ahead? Or you are feeling excited but need extra focus.

Choose an emotion or goal to work on for your morning tapping session.

2. Create a Set-Up Statement: Use a set-up statement that reflects your current emotional state or goal for the day. For example:
- ✓ *Even though I feel anxious about today, I deeply and completely accept myself."*
- ✓ *Even though I'm worried about this upcoming meeting, I deeply and completely accept myself."*
- ✓ *Even though I feel unfocused, I deeply and completely accept myself."*

3. Tap Through the Points: As you tap through the points, repeat a short phrase that captures the emotion or goal. For example, ***"This anxiety about today"*** or ***"This feeling of being unfocused."***

4. Introduce a Positive Intention: Once you have cleared any negative emotions, introduce a positive intention for the day. For example:

- ✓ *"I am calm, confident, and ready for a successful day."*
- ✓ *"I am focused and motivated to achieve my goals."*
- ✓ *"I trust that today will unfold in perfect alignment with my desires."*

5. Visualise Your Day: As you tap, take a moment to visualise your day going exactly as you want it to. See yourself managing tasks with ease, staying focused, and feeling positive. This helps reinforce your intention with emotional alignment.

Time Required: 5-10 minutes.

B. Midday Tapping: Releasing Stress and Refocusing

Checking in with oneself in the middle of the day is an excellent way to evaluate if any resistance or stress has accumulated. It is normal to run into obstacles or diversions during the day, so tapping briefly can help you decompress and get back on track.

Steps for Midday Tapping:

- Notice How You are Feeling: Take a moment to check in with yourself. Are you feeling stressed, frustrated, or overwhelmed? Or you are feeling disconnected from your goals? Find the primary emotion that is arising.

- Create a Set-Up Statement: Use a set-up statement that reflects the emotion you want to release.
For example:
- ✓ ***Even though I feel stressed about this project, I deeply and completely accept myself."***
- ✓ ***Even though I'm frustrated by how my day is going, I deeply and completely accept myself."***
- ✓ ***Even though I'm feeling distracted and unfocused, I deeply and completely accept myself."***

- **Tap Through the Points**: As you tap through the points, repeat a short reminder phrase that captures the emotion. For example, ***"This stress about the project"*** or ***"This frustration with my day."***

- **Refocus with Positive Affirmations:** Once the emotional intensity has decreased, introduce a positive affirmation that helps you refocus.

For example:
- ✓ *"I am calm, focused, and capable."*
- ✓ *"I trust that I can complete my tasks with ease."*
- ✓ *"I release any frustration and stay focused on what matters most."*

- **Return to Your Goals**: After tapping, take a few moments to refocus on your main goals for the day. This helps to realign your energy and stay on track.

Time Required: 5-10 minutes.

C. Evening Tapping: Reflecting and Letting Go

It is crucial to consider your feelings and experiences at the end of the day. Tapping in the evening eases the release of any tension, limiting beliefs, or residual emotions that may have surfaced during the day. This enables you to sleep with clarity and calm, which makes it simpler to keep an optimistic outlook.

Steps for Evening Tapping:

- **Reflect on Your Day:** Take a few moments to reflect on how your day went. Did any difficult emotions or limiting beliefs surface? Did you feel any stress or frustration that has not been fully resolved? Find the primary emotion you want to work on before bed.

- **Create a Set-Up Statement**: Use a set-up statement that reflects how you feel at the end of the day. For example:

- ✓ ***Even though I feel stressed about what happened today, I deeply and completely accept myself."***
- ✓ ***Even though I'm frustrated about not getting enough done, I deeply and completely accept myself."***
- ✓ ***Even though I still feel anxious about tomorrow, I deeply and completely accept myself."***

- **Tap Through the Points**: Tap through the sequence while repeating a short reminder phrase like ***"This stress from today"*** or ***"This frustration about not finishing my tasks."***

- **Let Go with Positive Affirmations:** Once you have cleared the emotional intensity, introduce a positive affirmation to help you let go and relax.

For example:

- ✓ *"I release all stress and tension from today."*
- ✓ *"I trust that everything is working out for my highest good."*
- ✓ *"I am calm and at peace, ready for a restful night's sleep."*

- Visualise the Next Day: As you tap, visualise yourself waking up the next day feeling refreshed, focused, and ready to embrace new opportunities. This helps you go to bed with a positive mindset and look forward to the day ahead.

Time Required: 10-15 minutes.

D. Using Tapping During Challenging Moments

You can employ tapping in real-time during challenging times in addition to your morning, lunchtime, and nightly routines. At any time during the day, if you feel overburdened, anxious, or emotionally agitated, take a moment to stand back and tap through the points.

Steps for Real-Time Tapping:

- Find the Emotion: Recognise the primary emotion you are feeling—whether it is anxiety, anger, frustration, or fear.

- Tap Through the Points: As you tap, focus on releasing the emotion in the moment. For example, ***"This anxiety about the situation"*** or ***"This anger I'm feeling right now."***

- Reframe the Situation: Once the emotional intensity has decreased, introduce a positive reframe or affirmation to help you manage the situation with more clarity and calm.

For example:
- ✓ *"I can handle this with ease."*

✓ *"I choose to stay calm and centred."*
✓ *"I trust that everything is working out."*

Tapping for even a short while during a demanding situation can help you feel less emotionally charged and handle the matter more calmly and clearly.

How to Stay Consistent with Your Daily Tapping Routine

Consistency is the key to success when it comes to tapping. The more regularly you practise, the easier it will become to stay emotionally clear and aligned with your goals. Here are a few tips to help you stay consistent with your daily tapping routine:

1. Schedule Tapping into Your Day: Treat tapping as a non-negotiable part of your day, just like brushing your teeth or eating breakfast. By scheduling time for tapping whether it is in the morning, during a break, or before bed you make it a regular habit.

2. Use Reminders: To remind yourself to tap, set reminders on your phone or make a visual sign (such as post it notes). This is particularly beneficial when you are just beginning your routine.

3. Start Small: If you are new to tapping, start with just 5 minutes a day. Once you have set up the habit, you can gradually increase the time as needed. Even a few minutes of tapping can make a significant difference.

4. Track Your Progress: Keep a journal or use a tracking app to record your tapping sessions. Note how you feel before and after each session and track any shifts in your emotional state or progress towards your goals. This helps to reinforce the positive impact of your practice.

5. Be Patient and Persistent: Change takes time, so be patient with yourself. Some emotional blocks may take longer to clear than others, and that is okay. Trust that with consistent tapping, you are making progress, even if it is not always at once noticeable.

Conclusion

Building a daily tapping routine is one of the most effective ways to stay emotionally aligned with your goals and ensure long-term success in manifestation. By dedicating just a few minutes each day to clearing emotional resistance and reinforcing positive beliefs, you create the mental and emotional space needed to manifest your desires more easily.

In the next chapter, we will discuss shared challenges that arise when using tapping for the Law of Attraction and how to overcome them. Whether you face doubts, emotional setbacks, or resistance, you will learn strategies to stay committed to your tapping practice and continue making progress towards your goals.

Chapter 11

Common Challenges and How to Overcome Them

Even while tapping is an effective method for removing emotional obstacles and strengthening the Law of Attraction, there may still be obstacles in your path. These challenges, which can include resistance, annoyance, or uncertainty, can make it more difficult to sustain a high vibratory state or to be consistent in your practice. Understanding how to find and go beyond these obstacles without allowing them to stop you from moving forward is essential to success with tapping and manifestation.

This chapter will discuss some of the most typical problems people run into when employing tapping for manifestation, as well as workable solutions. You may keep up a regular tapping practice, remain emotionally in line with your goals, and continue with your manifestation journey by knowing how to overcome these obstacles.

Challenge 1: Doubt and Scepticisms

One of the most familiar challenges people have when using tapping is doubt, especially if they are new to the technique. You may question whether tapping is effective or if it is too simple to succeed. This can be a significant barrier to your success because it creates emotional resistance and prevents you from giving the process your full attention.

Why Doubt Arises:

Doubt often arises from the belief that change needs to be complicated or difficult. If you have struggled with certain emotional or mental patterns for a long time, the idea that a technique as simple as tapping could help release them might seem unrealistic. Additionally, if you have tried other approaches that did not work, you might bring that scepticism into your tapping practice.

How to Overcome Doubt:

1. Start with Small Wins:

If you are feeling doubtful, try starting with a small, manageable issue. For example, tap on a minor annoyance or stress you are experiencing, rather than a deep-seated belief. By working on something small, you are more likely to see quick results, which can help build your confidence in tapping's effectiveness.

2. Keep a Journal of Progress:

Track your emotional shifts before and after tapping. Write down how you feel before you start a session and check in with yourself afterward. Over time, this will provide evidence of the changes you are experiencing, which can help reduce doubt and strengthen your belief in the process.

3. Commit to Consistency:

Many times, doubt stems from a lack of consistency. The more often you tap, the more improvements you will see. To get past your first cynicism, try committing to a daily tapping practice for a few weeks and see the slow emotional changes that take place.

4. Be Open to the Experience:

Have an open mind when tapping. Instead of worrying about whether it will succeed, just give yourself permission to take part in the process. Releasing the need for instant evidence or results might occasionally lessen resistance and enable the emotional changes to occur organically.

Challenge 2: Feeling Stuck or Blocked

Sometimes you could feel that you are trapped and that no matter how often you tap, nothing is changing. You may discover that you are not getting the desired outcomes or that some emotional problems do not appear to go away. This can lead to frustration and even cause you to doubt whether tapping is working at all.

Why You Might Feel Stuck:

Struggling with deeply ingrained beliefs or emotional patterns that have persisted for many years can often leave you feeling stuck. It is possible that these ideas have grown so embedded in your mind that they require more effort and time to overcome. Furthermore, feeling stuck may show that you are experiencing secondary gains, which are unintended advantages that come from clinging to a thought or emotional state—even if it is a bad one.

How to Overcome Feeling Stuck:

1. Address One Layer at a Time:

Deep-seated emotional issues are often multi-layered, and it is important to work through them gradually. Rather than trying to tackle everything at once, focus on one aspect of the issue at a time. For example, if you are tapping on a belief like ***"I'm not good enough,"*** you might break it down into smaller components, such as fear of failure, fear of rejection, or a specific experience that contributed to the belief. By addressing these smaller layers, you will gradually release the overall belief.

2. Be Patient with the Process:

Sometimes progress can feel slow, especially when dealing with long-standing emotional issues. Remind yourself that it took time for these beliefs and patterns to form, and it may take time to fully release them. Trust that even if the shifts feel small, you are making progress with each tapping session.

3. Find Secondary Gains:

Consider whether there is a secret reason you might be clinging to the thought or emotional state if you are feeling trapped. For instance, you may unconsciously think that stress keeps you motivated or that clinging to your fears keeps you safe. You may specifically tap into and release the benefits you are receiving once you have found these secondary gains.

4. Seek Support if Needed:

If you find that you are consistently feeling stuck, you might receive help from working with a qualified EFT practitioner. A practitioner can help you find blind spots, guide you through more complex issues, and offer added insight into why you might be struggling to make progress.

Challenge 3: Emotional Overwhelm

Tapping can bring up strong emotions, especially if you are working on a particularly intense issue or unresolved trauma. While this emotional release is part of the healing process, it can sometimes feel overwhelming, making you hesitant to continue your tapping practice.

Why Emotional Overwhelm Occurs:

When you tap on an emotional issue, you are bringing it to the surface, which can sometimes cause the emotions to feel more intense before they begin to release. This is known as an emotional crescendo a temporary increase in emotional intensity before the emotion dissipates. Overwhelm can also occur if you are tapping on multiple issues at once, leading to emotional overload.

How to Manage Emotional Overwhelm:

1. Focus on Safety and Grounding:

If you are feeling overwhelmed, it is important to ground yourself before continuing. Pause your tapping session and take a few deep breaths. You can also do some grounding exercises, such as visualising yourself rooted to the earth or tapping on calming affirmations like, *"I am safe, and I trust this process."*

2. Work Slowly and Gently:

When dealing with intense emotions, it is helpful to work slowly. Rather than diving straight into the most painful aspect of an issue, you can start by tapping around the edges. For example, if you are dealing with grief, you might begin by tapping on the feelings of heaviness or sadness, rather than focusing on the core of the grief at once.

3. Reduce the Emotional Intensity:

If you notice that your emotions are becoming too intense, you can reduce the intensity by tapping on more neutral or soothing phrases. For example, instead of focusing on the strong emotion itself, you might tap on phrases like, ***"It's okay to feel this way"*** or ***"I am doing the best I can to heal."***

4. Take Breaks When Needed:

It is perfectly okay to take breaks during a taping session. If the emotions become too overwhelming, pause the session, and come back to it later. Remember, healing is a process, and it is important to honour your emotional needs.

Challenge 4: Resistance to Change

Even when you consciously want to manifest your desires, you may meet subconscious resistance to change. This resistance can take many forms, such as procrastination, avoiding tapping sessions, or making excuses for why you cannot focus on your goals. This resistance can be frustrating, as it often shows up just when you are on the verge of a breakthrough.

Why Resistance to Change Happens:

Change can feel threatening to the subconscious mind, especially if you have been living with a particular belief or emotional pattern for a long time. Your mind might perceive the unknown success, love, or abundance as risky, even if it is what you want. As a result, you might unconsciously resist taking the actions necessary to create change, keeping yourself in a state of familiarity and comfort.

How to Overcome Resistance:

1. Tap on the Resistance Itself:

If you notice yourself resisting change, you can tap directly on that resistance.

For example:

✓ *Even though I'm resisting success, I deeply and completely accept myself."*

✓ *Even though I'm afraid of change, I deeply and completely accept myself."*

By tapping on the fear or discomfort around change, you can reduce the emotional intensity of the resistance and create space for new possibilities.

2. Focus on the Benefits of Change:

Sometimes resistance comes from focusing too much on the discomfort of change, rather than the benefits. After tapping on the resistance, shift your focus to the positive outcomes that change will bring.

Tap on affirmations like:

✓ *"I am excited for the new opportunities that success will bring."*

✓ *"I trust that this change is for my highest good."*

3. Start with Small Steps:

If the thought of tremendous changes feels overwhelming, start with small, manageable steps. Tap on one aspect of the change at a time and take incremental actions towards your goal. This gradual approach makes change feel less intimidating and helps reduce resistance.

4. Visualise Success:

Visualisation can be a powerful tool for overcoming resistance. After tapping, take a few moments to visualise yourself living the reality you want to create. See yourself enjoying the success, love, or abundance you want. This helps your subconscious mind feel more comfortable with the idea of change and reinforces your intention to move forward.

Challenge 5: Impatience with Results

Manifestation requires time, just like any other phase of progress. When you are working on major projects or emotional problems that have been bothering you for a long time, it is normal to feel impatient when you do not see results right away. Impatience, on the other hand, can lead to emotional resistance, which lowers your vibration and makes it more difficult for your goals to come true.

Why Impatience Arises:

Impatience often comes from the belief that results should happen quickly, or that if you do not see immediate changes, tapping is not working. This mindset can lead to frustration and a sense of discouragement, making it harder to stay consistent with your practice.

How to Manage Impatience:

1. Trust the Process:

Remind yourself that tapping and manifestation are processes, not instant fixes. Each tapping session contributes to your overall progress, even if the results are not at once visible. Trust that as you continue to clear emotional blocks, your manifestations are moving closer to reality.

2. Celebrate Small Wins:

Rather than focusing on the end goal, take time to celebrate the small shifts you experience along the way. Whether it is feeling less anxious, noticing a new opportunity, or having a small breakthrough, these wins are signs that you are making progress. Acknowledging these moments can help reduce impatience.

3. Tap on Impatience:

If you are feeling impatient, you can tap directly on that emotion.

For example:

- ✓ *Even though I feel impatient with my progress, I deeply and completely accept myself."*
- ✓ *Even though I'm frustrated that things aren't happening fast enough, I deeply and completely accept myself."*

Tapping on impatience helps to release the emotional charge and shift you back into a state of trust and flow.

4. Focus on the Present:

Focussing too much on the future and what has not happened yet might lead to impatience. After you have finished tapping, pause to focus on the here and now. Trust that every step you take will bring you closer to the result you want and concentrate on what you can do today to support your goals.

Conclusion

Any growth process inevitably involves challenges, but you do not have to let them keep you from reaching your aims. You may stay on course and keep using the Law of Attraction to your advantage by tapping to deal with impatience, resistance, doubt, and emotional overload. You become more emotionally resilient and more in line with your desires every time you conquer a difficulty.

We will look at actual success stories of people who have used tapping and the Law of Attraction to change their lives in the upcoming chapter. These tales will encourage and inspire you to persevere through difficulties, proving that anything is achievable with perseverance and the correct resources.

Chapter 12

Real-Life Success Stories: Manifesting with Tapping

One of the most inspiring aspects of combining tapping with the Law of Attraction is hearing about the real-life transformations people have experienced. While the process of manifestation often feels personal and internal, the success stories of others can offer valuable insight, motivation, and reassurance that these methods truly work. Everyone's journey is unique, but what unites them is the power of using tapping to overcome emotional blocks and align their energy with their desires.

In this chapter, we will explore a range of success stories from people who have used tapping to manifest their goals in areas such as financial abundance, relationships, health, and career success. These stories prove how consistent tapping can lead to profound emotional shifts, helping people break through limiting beliefs and achieve their dreams. As you read these examples, you may find parallels with your own challenges, and these stories will encourage you to stay committed to your tapping practice and trust in the process.

1. Sarah's Story: Manifesting Financial Freedom Background:

Sarah had always struggled with her finances. Despite working hard and earning a decent salary, she found herself living from paycheck to pay check. She carried a deep-seated belief that money was hard to come by and that no matter how much she earned, it would never be enough. This limiting belief had been reinforced since childhood, where money had always been a source of stress in her family. Sarah also felt guilty about wanting more money, as she had been taught that wanting wealth was greedy.

How Tapping Helped:

Sarah discovered tapping through a friend who had experienced financial breakthroughs using EFT. Initially sceptical, she decided to try it. She began tapping daily on her limiting beliefs around money, using set-up statements such as, ***"Even though I believe money is hard to come by, I deeply and completely accept myself,"*** and ***"Even though I feel guilty for wanting financial freedom, I deeply and completely accept myself."***
As she tapped, Sarah noticed emotional memories from her childhood surfacing memories of her parents arguing about money and her own feelings of lack as a child. She

continued tapping to release these emotional ties and to clear her guilt about wanting financial abundance.

Over time, Sarah replaced her old limiting beliefs with empowering affirmations like*, "I am worthy of financial abundance,"* and ***"Money flows to me easily and effortlessly."*** She visualised herself living in financial freedom, feeling secure and abundant.

The Outcome:

Within a few months of consistent tapping, Sarah experienced a dramatic shift in her financial situation. She received an unexpected job offer that significantly increased her income, and she felt more confident in managing her finances. The anxiety and fear she once associated with money disappeared, and she began attracting new opportunities for financial growth. Today, Sarah describes her relationship with money as peaceful and abundant, and she credits tapping with helping her reprogram her beliefs and manifest financial freedom.

2. James's Story:
Attracting a Loving Relationship Background:

James had been single for many years and was frustrated with his inability to attract a meaningful relationship. He had been through several heartbreaks in the past and had developed a fear of vulnerability, believing that love would always lead to pain. Despite his desire for companionship, he felt emotionally blocked and unworthy of finding true love.

How Tapping Helped:

After attending a workshop on tapping and the Law of Attraction, James decided to use EFT to address his fears around relationships. He began by tapping on his fear of vulnerability, using the set-up statement, ***"Even though I'm afraid of getting hurt again, I deeply and completely accept myself."*** As he tapped, he acknowledged the hurt and rejection from past relationships, and gradually, he felt those old wounds begin to heal.

James also tapped on his feelings of unworthiness, using affirmations like, ***"I am worthy of love and connection,"*** and ***"I attract loving, supportive relationships."*** He visualised himself in a healthy, fulfilling relationship, focusing on the positive emotions of love, trust, and joy.

The Outcome:

Within a few months, James noticed a significant shift in how he approached relationships. He no longer carried the same fear of vulnerability and began opening himself up to new experiences. Shortly after, he met someone who shared his values and desires, and they quickly formed a deep and meaningful relationship. James credits tapping with helping him release his emotional baggage from the past and align with the love he had always wanted.

3. Emma's Story:
Overcoming Health Challenges Background:

Emma had been struggling with chronic fatigue and frequent health issues for years. Despite trying various treatments, she often felt frustrated by the lack of progress and carried a sense of hopelessness about her body's ability to heal. She also had a deep-seated belief that "good health is difficult to maintain" and often felt anxious about her physical wellbeing.

How Tapping Helped:

Emma began using tapping to address the emotional aspects of her health challenges. She started with the set-up statement, ***"Even though I feel frustrated with my health, I deeply and completely accept myself."*** As she tapped, she acknowledged the frustration, fear, and anxiety she had been carrying about her body.

She also tapped on the belief that health was hard to keep, replacing it with affirmations such as, ***"I trust in my body's ability to heal,"*** and ***"My body is healthy, strong, and resilient."*** Emma made tapping part of her daily routine, focusing not only on her physical symptoms but also on the emotional patterns that had been contributing to her health issues.

The Outcome:

After several weeks of tapping, Emma noticed a significant improvement in her energy levels. She felt more in control of her health and no longer carried the same fear and frustration that had been weighing her down. Her physical symptoms began to ease, and she adopted a more positive and empowered mindset about her body's healing process. Today, Emma continues to use tapping as part of her comprehensive approach to keeping good health and wellbeing.

4. David's Story: Manifesting Career Success Background:

David had always felt stuck in his career. He worked in a job that he did not enjoy but felt too afraid to make a change. He carried a belief that success was only for other people and that he was not good enough to achieve his dreams. Despite his desire to start his own business, he procrastinated, doubted his abilities, and feared failure.

How Tapping Helped:

David decided to use tapping to address his limiting beliefs around success. He began with the set-up statement, ***"Even though I'm afraid of failing and believe success is not for me, I deeply and completely accept myself."*** As he tapped, he focused on the feelings of fear, self-doubt, and insecurity that had been holding him back.

He also introduced new affirmations, such as, ***"I am capable of achieving great success,"*** and ***"I trust in my abilities to create the career I desire."*** David used to tap to clear the fear of failure and procrastination that had been keeping him stuck.

The Outcome:

After several months of tapping, David felt a surge of confidence and motivation to pursue his goals. He finally took the leap and started his own business, which grew rapidly in the first year. His mindset shifted from fear of failure to one of empowerment and possibility, and he now enjoys the career of which he had always dreamed. David credits tapping with helping him break free from his limiting beliefs and take the bold steps necessary for success.

5. Rachel's Story: Manifesting Peace and Emotional Healing Background:

Rachel had struggled with anxiety and emotional overwhelm for most of her life. She often felt consumed by worry, fear, and self-doubt, and found it difficult to stay calm and grounded, even in everyday situations. These emotional patterns made it challenging for her to enjoy life fully or feel at peace.

How Tapping Helped:

Rachel discovered tapping to manage her anxiety. She began with the set-up statement, ***"Even though I feel anxious and overwhelmed, I deeply and completely accept myself."*** She tapped regularly to address her feelings of worry and fear, using affirmations like, ***"I am calm and at peace,"*** and ***"I trust that I am safe and supported."***

She also used to tap to address the root causes of her anxiety, including childhood experiences that had contributed to her emotional patterns. By working through these emotional layers, Rachel was able to release much of the fear and tension that had been weighing her down.

The Outcome:

Over time, Rachel experienced a profound shift in her emotional wellbeing. She no longer felt overwhelmed by anxiety and learned to manage her emotions with greater ease. Tapping helped her find a sense of inner peace and emotional balance, and she now feels more empowered to handle life's challenges with calm and confidence. Rachel continues to use tapping as a daily practice to keep her emotional health.

Key Lessons from These Success Stories

These real-life success stories illustrate several key lessons about the power of tapping and the Law of Attraction:

1. Consistent Practice Yields Results:

Each of these individuals committed to tapping on a regular basis, making it part of their daily routine. This consistency allowed them to clear deep emotional blocks and gradually shift their mindset and energy. Even when progress seemed slow, persistence paid off.

2. Emotional Blocks Often Run Deep:
Limiting beliefs and emotional patterns are often rooted in past experiences, sometimes going back to childhood. By using tapping to address these deeper emotional layers, the individuals in these stories were able to create lasting change in their beliefs, emotions, and behaviour.

3. Tapping Helps Create Emotional Alignment:
The power of the Law of Attraction lies in emotional alignment—feeling as though your desires have already manifested. Through tapping, these individuals were able to release the negative emotions that were blocking their desires and replace them with positive emotions that aligned with their goals.

4. Tapping Transforms Both the Inner and Outer World:
As these individuals worked through their emotional blocks, they noticed shifts not only in how they felt but also in their outer reality. New opportunities, relationships, and experiences began to flow into their lives as they aligned their energy with their desires.

Conclusion
These success stories serve as powerful reminders that tapping, when combined with the Law of Attraction, can lead to profound transformation in all areas of life. Whether you are looking to improve your health, attract financial abundance, find love, or achieve career success, tapping can help you

clear the emotional resistance that stands in the way and open the door to new possibilities.

In the next chapter, we will explore how to combine tapping with visualisation and meditation to create an even more powerful manifestation practice. You will learn how to integrate these techniques to amplify your emotional alignment and accelerate the manifestation process.

Chapter 13

Combining Tapping with Visualisation and Meditation

While tapping is an incredibly powerful tool on its own, its effectiveness can be amplified when combined with other techniques such as visualisation and meditation. Both practices work harmoniously with tapping to deepen your connection to your desires and strengthen your emotional alignment with your goals. By integrating tapping with visualisation and meditation, you create a comprehensive approach to manifestation that engages both the mind and the body, helping you tap into your full potential.

In this chapter, we will explore how to combine tapping with visualisation and meditation to enhance the Law of Attraction. You will learn how each technique complements the other, and how to create a powerful daily practice that accelerates your manifestation journey. By the end of this chapter, you will have the tools to use these techniques together to amplify your results and make manifestation an even more transformative experience.

The Power of Visualisation

Visualisation is a widely used technique in the manifestation process. It involves imagining yourself already living the life you want, experiencing the emotions, situations, and success that you want to attract. Visualisation helps you align your thoughts and feelings with your goals, allowing your subconscious mind to start accepting these desires as your reality.

When you combine visualisation with tapping, you not only create a vivid mental image of your desired outcomes but also clear any emotional or energetic blocks that may prevent you from believing in or achieving those outcomes. Tapping prepares the mind and body by releasing resistance, while visualisation strengthens the emotional connection to your goals. This combination allows you to experience the emotional and energetic frequency of your desires as though they have already manifested.

How to Use Tapping and Visualisation Together

Here is a step-by-step guide on how to combine tapping with visualisation for a more powerful manifestation practice:

1. Start by Tapping to Clear Resistance

Before you begin your visualisation, start with a round of tapping to clear any negative emotions or limiting beliefs that might block your ability to focus or feel aligned with your desires. For example, if you are trying to manifest financial abundance but feel anxious about money, begin by tapping on that anxiety.

Use a set-up statement such as:

- ✓ *Even though I feel anxious about money, I deeply and completely accept myself."*
- ✓ *Even though I'm worried about my financial situation, I deeply and completely accept myself."*

As you tap through the points, repeat a short reminder phrase like **"This anxiety about money"** or **"This fear of financial insecurity."** Continue tapping until the emotional intensity of the issue has lessened.

2. Introduce Positive Affirmations

After tapping on the negative emotion, introduce a positive affirmation that aligns with your desire.
For example:

- ✓ *"I am open to receiving financial abundance."*
- ✓ *"Money flows to me easily and effortlessly."*

Tap through the sequence again while focusing on these affirmations. This helps to reframe your mindset and prepare you for the next step—visualisation.

3. Begin Your Visualisation

Once you have tapped on the resistance and introduced a positive affirmation, close your eyes, and begin to visualise your desired outcome. For example, if you are visualising financial abundance, imagine yourself living in a state of financial freedom. See yourself having more than enough money to meet your needs and desires, feeling secure, and enjoying the wealth that flows to you.

Focus on the emotions of already having what you want. How do you feel in this new reality? Experience the joy, gratitude, confidence, or excitement that comes with your success. The more vividly you can imagine the scene, the more powerful your visualisation will be.

4. Combine Tapping with Visualisation

As you visualise, continue tapping through the points to further integrate the emotions you are experiencing. For example, while visualising yourself in financial abundance, tap through the points and repeat phrases such as:

- ✓ *"I am so grateful for the financial freedom I now have."*
- ✓ *"I feel secure and confident in my financial future."*
- ✓ *"I love how money flows to me easily."*

Tapping while visualising helps to anchor these positive emotions and beliefs into your energy system, making them feel more real and achievable.

5. End with a Final Round of Tapping

After completing your visualisation, end with a final round of tapping to solidify the emotional alignment you have created.

You can repeat affirmations like:
- ✓ *"I am aligned with the energy of abundance."*

✓ *"I trust that my desires are manifesting in perfect timing."*
✓ *"I am open and ready to receive."*

This final round helps reinforce the positive emotions and ensures that you stay in a high-vibrational state after the session.

How Long Should You Spend on Visualisation and Tapping?

You do not need to spend a lot of time on these sessions to see results. A **10–15-minute** practice combining tapping and visualisation can be incredibly effective. The key is consistency doing this daily or several times a week will keep your energy aligned with your desires and help you manifest more easily.

The Benefits of Combining Tapping with Visualisation

- **Clearing Emotional Resistance:** Tapping helps to remove the emotional blocks that can prevent you from fully embracing your visualisation. By clearing negative emotions first, you can focus more deeply on positive outcomes during the visualisation.

- **Strengthening Emotional Alignment:** Visualisation allows you to experience the emotions of your desired outcome, and tapping helps to integrate those emotions more fully into your energy system. This creates a deeper sense of alignment with your goals.

- Anchoring New Beliefs: As you combine tapping and visualisation, you do not only imagine your success, but you are also rewiring your subconscious mind to accept it as possible. This helps replace old limiting beliefs with new, empowering ones that support your goals.

The Role of Meditation in Manifestation

Meditation is another powerful practice that can enhance your tapping and manifestation routine. While visualisation focuses on creating a mental image of your desired outcome, meditation helps you develop greater mental clarity, emotional calm, and a stronger connection to your intuition. Meditation allows you to quiet the mind, reduce stress, and access a deeper level of consciousness, where you can connect with the energy of the universe and your desires.

When combined with tapping, meditation becomes an even more powerful tool for manifestation. Tapping clears the emotional blocks that can create mental chatter or stress, while meditation helps you cultivate a sense of inner peace and stillness. This combination allows you to enter a state of flow, where you are more open to receiving insights, inspiration, and intuitive guidance.

How to Combine Tapping with Meditation

Here is a simple process for combining tapping with meditation to enhance your manifestation practice:

1. Start with Tapping to Release Tension

Before you begin meditating, do a quick round of tapping to release any tension, stress, or negative emotions. For example, you might tap on feelings of anxiety, impatience, or frustration.

Use a set-up statement like:

- ✓ ***Even though I feel stressed, I deeply and completely accept myself."***
- ✓ ***Even though I'm feeling impatient about my goals, I deeply and completely accept myself."***

As you tap, focus on letting go of any mental or emotional distractions that could interfere with your meditation.

2. Begin Your Meditation

Once you have cleared any emotional resistance, begin your meditation. You can use a simple mindfulness meditation, where you focus on your breath and allow thoughts to pass without attachment, or you can use a guided meditation that focuses on manifestation. The key is to cultivate a state of inner calm and presence.

3. Focus on Your Desired Outcome

As you enter a meditative state, bring your desired outcome to mind. However, rather than visualising in detail, simply focus on the feeling of having already achieved your goal. For example, if you are manifesting a new career opportunity, focus on the feeling of fulfilment, success, and excitement that comes with that achievement. Allow these feelings to wash over you as you meditate.

4. Use Tapping to Anchor the Emotions

After your meditation, finish with another round of tapping to anchor the positive emotions and sense of alignment you have cultivated.

Tap through the points while repeating affirmations such as:

- ✓ *"I am at peace, knowing that my desires are manifesting."*
- ✓ *"I trust in the universe's perfect timing."*
- ✓ *"I am aligned with the energy of my goals."*

This final round of tapping helps to reinforce the sense of calm and alignment you achieved during your meditation, making it easier to carry that energy into the rest of your day.

The Benefits of Combining Tapping with Meditation

- Enhanced Mental Clarity: Meditation helps clear mental clutter, allowing you to focus more effectively on your goals. Tapping before meditation ensures that any emotional distractions are cleared away, making your meditation deeper and more focused.

- Increased Emotional Calm: Meditation cultivates a sense of inner peace, while tapping releases emotional resistance. Together, these practices help you keep a calm, balanced emotional state that is essential for successful manifestation.

- Stronger Connection to Intuition: Meditation strengthens your connection to your intuition and inner guidance, helping you make decisions and take inspired action towards your goals. Tapping helps remove any fears or doubts that might block your connection to this intuitive wisdom.

- Greater Sense of Trust and Flow: Combining tapping and meditation helps you develop a sense of trust in the manifestation process. Tapping clears the resistance, while meditation helps you surrender and trust in the flow of the universe.

Creating a Daily Practice with Tapping, Visualisation, and Meditation

To get the most out of these techniques, it is helpful to create a daily practice that incorporates tapping, visualisation, and meditation. Here is a sample routine you can use:

1. Morning Tapping and Visualisation (10-15 minutes)

Start your day with a tapping session to clear any resistance and set your intentions. Follow this with a short visualisation where you imagine yourself achieving your goals. Focus on the emotions you want to feel throughout the day—whether it is confidence, abundance, or joy.

2. Midday Tapping (5-10 minutes)

If you meet stress or emotional resistance during the day, take a few minutes to tap through the points and release any negative emotions. This helps to keep your energy clear and aligned with your goals.

3. Evening Meditation and Tapping (10-15 minutes)

End your day with a short meditation to calm your mind and reflect on your progress. After meditating, do a final round of tapping to reinforce the positive emotions you have cultivated and release any lingering stress or resistance.

By combining these practices, you will create a powerful daily routine that helps you stay emotionally clear, mentally focused, and energetically aligned with your desires.

Conclusion

Combining tapping with visualisation and meditation creates a synergistic effect that enhances your ability to manifest your desires. While tapping helps to clear emotional and mental blocks, visualisation deepens your emotional connection to your goals, and meditation cultivates inner peace and clarity. Together, these practices offer a comprehensive approach to manifestation that engages both your mind and body, allowing you to align more fully with the energy of what you want to create.

In the next chapter, we will explore advanced tapping techniques for deep healing, where we will dive into more complex methods for addressing deeply ingrained emotional blocks and trauma. You will learn how to use tapping to work through more challenging issues, creating space for profound emotional and spiritual growth.

Top of Head
Eyebrow
Side of Eye
Under Eye
Under Nose
Under Mouth
Collarbone
Under Arm
Side of Hand

Chapter 14

Advanced Tapping Techniques for Deep Healing

As you progress with tapping, you may find that certain emotional blocks or limiting beliefs are more deeply ingrained than others. These blocks often stem from long-standing patterns, unresolved trauma, or deeply rooted fears that have been present for years, if not decades. While regular tapping is effective for clearing many of these issues, more complex emotional layers may require advanced tapping techniques for deeper healing.

In this chapter, we will explore advanced methods for using tapping to address deeply embedded emotional wounds, trauma, and ingrained patterns of thinking. These techniques are designed to go beyond surface-level emotions and help you access the core of your unresolved issues.

By working through these deeper layers, you can experience more profound emotional freedom and spiritual growth, clearing the way for greater success with the Law of Attraction.

Understanding Deep Emotional Blocks

Deep emotional blocks often arise from significant past experiences, such as childhood trauma, major life changes, or unresolved grief. These blocks become embedded in the subconscious mind and can manifest as chronic feelings of fear, guilt, shame, or unworthiness. When left unaddressed, these emotions can prevent you from fully manifesting your desires, no matter how much effort you put into positive thinking or goal setting.

These deep blocks may include:

- **Trauma from past relationships or emotional abuse:** Feelings of betrayal, rejection, or abandonment that may prevent you from forming healthy relationships or trusting others.

- **Childhood conditioning:** Messages you received as a child about your worth, abilities, or place in the world that have shaped your self-image and confidence in adulthood.

- **Unresolved grief or loss:** Deep emotional pain from losing a loved one or experiencing a significant life change that you have not fully processed.

- **Fear of failure or success:** Deep-seated fears related to stepping into your full potential, often linked to a fear of being judged or rejected.

Why Advanced Tapping is Needed for Deeper Healing

While regular tapping is effective for releasing many emotions, deeply embedded issues often require a more nuanced approach. Advanced tapping techniques help you access and release the underlying layers of emotions that may not be at once obvious or accessible with surface-level tapping. These techniques allow you to explore deeper emotions gently and safely, helping to release them at their root.

Advanced tapping techniques are particularly useful for:

- **Addressing complex trauma**: When trauma has created a web of interconnected emotions and beliefs, advanced tapping can help unravel these layers in a way that is both effective and healing.

- **Breaking repetitive patterns**: If you find yourself repeating the same emotional or behavioural patterns, advanced tapping can help you find and clear the subconscious programming that keeps you stuck.

- **Healing deeply ingrained beliefs**: Advanced techniques can be used to work through long-standing limiting beliefs that have been part of your self-image for many years.

Advanced Tapping Technique 1:

The Movie Technique

The Movie Technique is a powerful way to address traumatic memories or difficult past experiences. This method allows you to approach emotional pain or trauma without becoming overwhelmed, as it encourages you to "watch" the memory as though it were a movie, rather than reliving it. By taking a step back and tapping on the emotions that arise as you watch the memory unfold, you can process the trauma in a safe and controlled way.

How to Use the Movie Technique:

1. **Choose a Memory:** Start by selecting a memory or past event that causes emotional discomfort. It could be an argument, a breakup, or a specific event from childhood. Make sure it is an event you are ready to work on, and if the memory is highly traumatic, consider seeking support from an **EFT** practitioner.

2. **Rate the Emotional Intensity:** Before you begin tapping, rate the emotional intensity of the memory on a scale of **0 to 10**, with ten being the most intense. This will help you track your progress.

3. **Describe the Memory Like a Movie:** Imagine the memory as a movie or short film. Briefly describe the event in a few sentences, as though you are watching it unfold on a

screen. For example, "I'm watching myself argue with my partner. I feel hurt and angry."

4. Tap on the Emotional Charge: As you "watch" the movie, notice the emotions that come up—whether it is anger, sadness, fear, or frustration. Tap on the points while focusing on the emotion, using a set-up statement like*, "Even though I feel hurt and angry watching this memory, I deeply and completely accept myself."* Continue tapping through the points while you describe each scene of the memory.

5. Pause and Check the Intensity: After a round of tapping, pause and check how intense the memory feels now. Has the emotional charge decreased? If it is still strong, continue tapping on various aspects of the memory until the intensity comes down to a manageable level.

6. Repeat Until the Memory Feels Neutral: Continue using the Movie Technique until you can "watch" the memory without feeling a strong emotional response. The goal is not to erase the memory but to neutralise its emotional charge so that it no longer triggers negative feelings.

7. Introduce Positive Reframes: Once the emotional charge has lessened, you can introduce positive affirmations or new perspectives. For example, *"I've learned from this experience, and I'm stronger now,"* or *"I forgive myself and others involved in this memory."*

Advanced Tapping Technique 2:

The Tell the Story Technique

The Tell the Story Technique is like the Movie Technique, but instead of visualising the memory like a film, you verbally tell the story of the event while tapping. This technique allows you to work through the emotions in a step-by-step way, addressing each aspect of the story and clearing any emotional intensity as it arises.

How to Use the Tell the Story Technique:

1. **Choose a Distressing Memory:** Select a memory or event that causes emotional discomfort. It might be something from your past that still bothers you, like an argument, a loss, or a traumatic incident.

2. **Rate the Emotional Intensity:** Before you begin, rate how intense the memory feels on a scale of 0 to 10.

3. **Tell the Story in Sections:** Begin telling the story of the event aloud, starting with the first scene. For example, ***"It started when my friend said something that hurt me."*** As you tell each part of the story, notice any emotions that come up—whether it is sadness, anger, or anxiety.

4. **Tap on Each Emotion:** As you describe the first scene, tap on the points while focusing on the emotions that arise. Use a set-up statement like, ***"Even though I feel angry remembering this, I deeply and completely accept***

myself." Continue tapping through the points while you tell this part of the story.

5. Pause and Check the Emotional Intensity: After tapping on one section of the story, pause and check the intensity of your emotions. Has the emotional charge decreased? If not, continue tapping until the emotions around that part of the story feel less intense.

6. Move to the Next Section: Once the first part of the story feels neutral, move on to the next section.

For example, ***"Then I remember feeling really upset because my friend didn't understand me."*** Tap on the emotions that come up and continue telling the story in small sections.

7. Repeat Until the Entire Story Feels Neutral: Continue telling and tapping through the entire story until you can recount the memory without feeling a strong emotional response. The aim is to process the memory in a step-by-step way, reducing the emotional charge with each round of tapping.

8. Reframe the Story: Once you have worked through the emotional charge, you can reframe the story with a more positive or empowering perspective. For example, ***"I handled that situation the best I could at the time,"*** or ***"I've grown stronger since this event."***

Advanced Tapping Technique 3:

Chasing the Pain

Chasing the Pain is an advanced tapping technique used to address physical discomfort that may be linked to emotional issues. Many physical symptoms—such as chronic pain, headaches, or tension—can have emotional roots. By "chasing" the pain with tapping, you can help release the underlying emotions that contribute to physical discomfort.

How to Use Chasing the Pain:

1. **Focus on the Pain**: Begin by focusing on the physical sensation or pain in your body. Notice where the pain is found and how it feels—whether it's sharp, dull, throbbing, or tense.

2. **Rate the Pain Intensity:** Rate the intensity of the pain on a scale **of 0 to 10.**

3. **Tap on the Pain:** Use a set-up statement that acknowledges the pain, such as, ***"Even though I feel this pain in my back, I deeply and completely accept myself."*** As you tap through the points, focus on the sensation of the pain and any emotions that might be connected to it.

4. **Follow the Pain as It Moves:** As you tap, you may notice that the pain shifts or moves to a different part of your body. For example, you might start with pain in your back, and then notice that it moves to your shoulders or neck. This

is a sign that the emotional energy linked to the pain is shifting.

5. Chase the Pain: Continue tapping on the new location of the pain, using a set-up statement that reflects the shift, such as, ***"Even though the pain has moved to my shoulders, I deeply and completely accept myself."*** Follow the pain wherever it goes, tapping on each new sensation or emotion that arises.

6. Tap on Any Associated Emotions: As you chase the pain, notice if any emotions come up.

Often, physical pain is linked to emotions such as stress, anger, or sadness. Tap on these emotions as they arise, using set-up statements like, ***"Even though I feel stressed about this situation, I deeply and completely accept myself."***

7. Check for Emotional Shifts: After a few rounds of tapping, check to see if the intensity of the pain has decreased. You may also notice emotional shifts, such as feeling calmer or more relaxed. Continue tapping until both the physical and emotional discomfort have lessened.

Advanced Tapping Technique 4:

Matrix Reimprinting

Matrix Reimprinting is a more advanced technique that integrates **EFT** with visualisation to work on healing past trauma and negative memories. It is based on the idea that unresolved emotional pain gets **"stored"** in the energy field as ECHOES —representations of your younger self or past experiences that are stuck in emotional distress. By using tapping and visualisation, you can **"reimprint"** these memories with positive outcomes, helping to resolve the emotional charge and transform the memory.

How to Use Matrix Reimprinting:

1. **Identify a Distressing Memory:** Choose a past memory that carries emotional pain or discomfort. It could be a childhood memory, a relationship issue, or a traumatic experience.

2. **Visualise the Memory:** Close your eyes and visualise the memory, seeing your younger self or the version of you that experienced the event. This visualisation is your ECHO —the part of you that is still holding on to the emotional pain.

3. **Tap on the ECHO:** As you visualise the memory, imagine tapping on your younger self (the ECHO) to calm and soothe the emotions they are experiencing. Use a set-up

statement like, ***"Even though this part of me feels scared and alone, I deeply and completely accept them."***

4. Reimprint the Memory: Once the emotional intensity of the memory has decreased, reimprint the memory with a positive outcome. Visualise a new version of the event where you feel safe, supported, and empowered. Imagine yourself receiving comfort, love, or understanding from others in the memory.

5. Anchor the Positive Emotions: As you reimprint the memory, focus on the positive emotions you are experiencing—whether it is relief, happiness, or empowerment. Tap through the points while reinforcing these positive emotions, using affirmations like, ***"I am safe and supported"*** or ***"I have the power to create a positive future."***

Conclusion

Advanced tapping techniques provide you with the tools to address deeper emotional layers, heal past trauma, and release long-standing limiting beliefs. Whether you are using the Movie Technique, the Tell the Story Technique, Chasing the Pain, or Matrix Reimprinting, these methods allow you to access and clear the root causes of emotional distress, creating space for profound healing and growth.

As you explore these techniques, remember that healing is a journey. Some issues may require time and patience to fully resolve, but by consistently using tapping to address both surface-level and deeper emotional blocks, you will experience greater emotional freedom and alignment with your desires.

In the next chapter, we will conclude this book with a reflection on how to embrace your manifestation journey fully and continue evolving your practice with tapping and the Law of Attraction. You will learn how to stay committed to your goals, deepen your emotional alignment, and trust the unfolding of your desires.

Chapter 15

Conclusion: Embracing a New Manifestation Journey

As you come to the end of this guide on using tapping for the Law of Attraction, it is important to reflect on the powerful tools and techniques you have learned and how they can continue to support your journey. Manifestation is not a one-time event, but an ongoing process of personal growth, emotional alignment, and conscious creation. By consistently applying the methods you have explored in this book, you are embarking on a transformative path—one where you take control of your inner world and, as a result, see changes in your outer reality.

In this final chapter, we will discuss how to integrate what you've learned into your daily life, the importance of keeping a long-term tapping practice, and how to continue evolving your approach to manifesting. You will also discover how to stay connected to your goals and desires, even when challenges arise, and how to embrace a mindset of trust, patience, and openness as you move forward on your manifestation journey.

Tapping as a Lifelong Practice

Throughout this book, we have explored how tapping helps to release emotional blocks, reprogram limiting beliefs, and align your energy with your desires. What makes tapping so effective is its simplicity and adaptability—no matter what stage of life you are in or what challenges you are facing, you can always turn to tapping to clear resistance and reset your emotional state.

As you move forward, consider tapping not just as a tool for short-term manifestations, but as a lifelong practice for keeping emotional balance and inner peace. The more consistently you use tapping, the more easily you will be able to navigate life's difficulties without becoming stuck in negative patterns or limiting beliefs.

How to Maintain a Long-Term Tapping Practice:

1. Schedule Regular Tapping Sessions:

Make tapping part of your daily routine, just like brushing your teeth or exercising. Whether it is a short session in the morning to set your intentions, or a longer session in the evening to release the day's stress, regular tapping keeps your energy clear and aligned with your goals.

2. Tap on New Challenges as They Arise:
Life is constantly evolving, and new challenges will inevitably arise. Use tapping to address any emotional or mental blocks that come up in response to these changes. Whether it is a new goal you are working on, a difficult decision, or an unexpected setback, tapping helps you stay grounded and emotionally resilient.

3. Journal Your Progress:
Keep track of your tapping sessions and any emotional shifts you experience. Journaling helps you stay aware of your growth and reinforces the progress you are making. It also provides a space to reflect on any new insights or breakthroughs that come up during your practice.

4. Revisit Old Issues if Necessary:
Sometimes, old emotional wounds or limiting beliefs may resurface as you continue your journey. If this happens, do not be discouraged. Revisit these issues with tapping and see if there are deeper layers that need to be addressed. Each round of tapping brings you closer to full emotional freedom.

Trusting the Manifestation Process

One of the most important elements of manifesting with the Law of Attraction is trust—trust in yourself, in the universe, and in the process. Trust allows you to let go of the need to control every detail and instead focus on aligning your energy with your desires. It is easy to feel impatient when you do not see immediate results, but trusting the process means knowing that your desires are unfolding in perfect timing, even if you cannot see the full picture yet.

How to Cultivate Trust in the Process:

1. **Let Go of Attachment to the Outcome**:
   While it is important to be clear about what you want to manifest, it is equally important to release attachment to how and when it will happen. Tapping can help you release this attachment, allowing you to surrender to the process and trust that the universe is working in your favour.

2. **Focus on Emotional Alignment, Not Just Results:**
   Rather than fixating on the external results of your manifestations, focus on keeping emotional alignment. The more aligned you are with the feelings of joy, abundance, or love, the more easily these experiences will manifest in your reality. Use tapping to clear any resistance that takes you out of alignment, and trust that the results will follow naturally.

3. **Stay Open to Unexpected Opportunities:**
   Manifestation rarely unfolds exactly as we expect. The universe may deliver your desires in ways you had not imagined, or it may present opportunities that lead you in new directions. Stay open to these possibilities, and use tapping to release any fear or doubt that arises when things do not go according to your original plan.

4. **Celebrate Small Wins:**
   Every step towards your goal is worth celebrating. Whether it is a new opportunity, a shift in mindset, or an

emotional breakthrough, recognise the progress you are making. Celebrating small wins helps to reinforce the positive energy of your journey and keeps you motivated to continue.

Embracing Patience and Persistence

Manifestation is not always a linear process, and sometimes it can take longer than expected for your desires to materialise. In these moments, it is essential to embrace both patience and persistence. Patience allows you to stay calm and centred, even when results seem delayed, while persistence ensures that you keep moving forward towards your goals, even when faced with challenges.

How to Cultivate Patience and Persistence:

1. Remember That Growth Takes Time:
Just as plants take time to grow and bear fruit, your manifestations need time to develop. Trust that each step you take is moving you closer to your goals, even if the results are not at once visible. Use tapping to release any feelings of impatience and remind yourself that the process is unfolding in its own perfect timing.

2. Stay Committed to Your Practice:
Consistency is key to manifesting your desires. Even when progress seems slow, stay committed to your tapping practice and other manifestation techniques. Each session brings you closer to emotional freedom and alignment with your goals.

3. Tap on Setbacks:

Setbacks and obstacles are a natural part of any journey, but they do not have to derail your progress. When you meet challenges, use tapping to release any frustration, disappointment, or doubt that comes up. Tapping helps you reframe setbacks as opportunities for growth, allowing you to stay focused on your end goal.

4. Trust the Bigger Picture:

Sometimes, what is a delay or obstacle is part of a larger plan that is leading you towards an even better outcome than you imagined. Trust that the universe is always working behind the scenes, aligning the right people, opportunities, and circumstances to bring your desires to fruition.

Continuing Your Evolution with Tapping and the Law of Attraction

As you continue your manifestation journey, remember that both tapping and the Law of Attraction are tools for ongoing personal evolution. The more you tap, the more you clear old emotional patterns and make space for new experiences, insights, and growth. Manifestation is not just about achieving external goals—it is about becoming the best version of yourself and aligning with your highest potential.

Ways to Continue Evolving Your Practice:

1. Explore New Areas of Manifestation:

Once you have manifested success in one area of your life—whether it is health, wealth, relationships, or career—consider expanding your goals to new areas. Tapping can help you explore and manifest new desires as you continue to grow and evolve.

2. Deepen Your Emotional Awareness:

As you become more familiar with tapping, you will also become more attuned to your emotions. Continue using tapping to deepen your emotional awareness and clear any lingering blocks or unresolved issues. The more emotionally aligned you are, the more easily you can manifest your desires.

3. Experiment with New Manifestation Techniques:

While tapping is a powerful tool, there are many other manifestation techniques you can explore, such as affirmations, gratitude practices, or visualisation. Experiment with different methods to see what resonates with you and enhances your manifestation journey.

4. Trust in Your Ability to Create:

The most important lesson of all is to trust in your own ability to create the life you wish. You have the power to shape your reality through your thoughts, emotions, and energy. Tapping helps you align with this power and clear away any doubts or fears that might hold you back.

Embracing the Journey Ahead

Manifestation is not just about reaching a destination it is about enjoying the journey and embracing each step along the way. There will be moments of joy and success, as well as challenges and setbacks, but each experience offers an opportunity for growth and transformation. By using tapping to clear emotional blocks and align with your desires, you are creating a life filled with purpose, possibility, and abundance.

As you move forward, keep your focus on what truly matters to you. Stay committed to your goals, trust the process, and use the tools you have learned in this book to navigate your emotional landscape with clarity and confidence. With tapping and the Law of Attraction as your allies, there is no limit to what you can create.

Next Volume 2

200 Tapping set-up statements for all categories.

Example:
Emotional Wellbeing

Anxiety:

Here are five individual tapping set-up statements and full tapping sequences for addressing anxiety. These sequences will help you calm your nervous system, release fear, and reduce anxiety, whether it is generalised anxiety or anxiety about a specific situation. Follow each sequence by tapping through all the points, using the set-up statements and affirmations provided.

Tapping Points Overview

For each tapping round, you will tap on the following points:

1. **Karate Chop** (side of the hand)
2. **Eyebrow** (beginning of the brow, near the nose)
3. **Side of the Eye** (on the bone beside the eye)
4. **Under the Eye** (on the bone beneath the eye)
5. **Under the Nose** (between the nose and upper lip)
6. **Chin** (in the crease below the bottom lip)
7. **Collarbone** (just below the collarbone)
8. **Under the Arm** (about four inches below the armpit)
9. **Top of the Head** (crown of the head)

1. Generalised Anxiety

Set-Up Statement: (While tapping the karate chop point):

✓ ***"Even though I feel anxious and overwhelmed right now, I deeply and completely accept myself."***

Tapping Sequence:
- Eyebrow: "This anxiety I feel."
- Side of the Eye: "I feel so overwhelmed."
- Under the Eye: "This anxiety in my body."
- Under the Nose: "I'm worried and stressed."
- Chin: "I feel tension in my chest."
- Collarbone: "This anxious feeling."
- Under the Arm: "It's hard to relax."
- Top of the Head: "I feel anxious and uneasy."

Affirmations (Second Round):
- Eyebrow: "I choose to feel calm now."
- Side of the Eye: "I am safe in this moment."
- Under the Eye: "I can let go of this anxiety."
- Under the Nose: "I am finding peace within."
- Chin: "I am releasing this anxiety."
- Collarbone: "I feel more relaxed now."
- Under the Arm: "I trust that I can manage this."
- Top of the Head: "I am calm and in control."

2. Anxiety About the Future

Set-Up Statement: (While tapping the karate chop point):

✓ ***"Even though I'm anxious about the future and what might happen, I deeply and completely accept myself."***

Tapping Sequence:
- Eyebrow: "I'm worried about the future."
- Side of the Eye: "I don't know what's going to happen."
- Under the Eye: "I feel anxious about what's ahead."
- Under the Nose: "It's hard to feel in control."
- Chin: "I keep thinking about all the 'what ifs."
- Collarbone: "This fear of the unknown."
- Under the Arm: "I feel so tense."
- Top of the Head: "I'm anxious about what might happen."

Affirmations (Second Round):
- Eyebrow: "I choose to trust the process."

- Side of the Eye: "I release my fear of the unknown."
- Under the Eye: "I am safe right now."
- Under the Nose: "I trust that everything is working out."
- Chin: "I can manage whatever comes my way."
- Collarbone: "I release my need to control the future."
- Under the Arm: "I choose peace and calm now."
- Top of the Head: "I trust in the flow of life."

3. Anxiety in Social Situations

Set-Up Statement: (While tapping the karate chop point):

✓ ***"Even though I feel anxious in social situations and worry about what others think of me, I deeply and completely accept myself."***

Tapping Sequence:
- Eyebrow: "I feel so anxious in social situations."
- Side of the Eye: "I worry about what people think."
- Under the Eye: "This anxiety around others."
- Under the Nose: "I'm afraid I'll say or do the wrong thing."
- Chin: "I feel nervous and self-conscious."
- Collarbone: "I want to avoid these situations."
- Under the Arm: "This anxiety makes me feel small."
- Top of the Head: "I'm worried about being judged."

Affirmations (Second Round):
- Eyebrow: "I choose to feel calm around others."
- Side of the Eye: "I am worthy of being myself."
- Under the Eye: "I release my fear of judgment."
- Under the Nose: "I am confident and relaxed."

- Chin: "I trust that I'm good enough."
- Collarbone: "I choose to be at ease in social situations."
- Under the Arm: "I feel calm and comfortable now."
- Top of the Head: "I can relax and be myself."

4. Anxiety About Health

Set-Up Statement: (While tapping the karate chop point):

✓ ***"Even though I feel anxious about my health and worry something might go wrong, I deeply and completely accept myself."***

Tapping Sequence:
- Eyebrow: "I'm worried about my health."
- Side of the Eye: "I fear that something's wrong."
- Under the Eye: "I feel anxious about my body."
- Under the Nose: "I keep thinking about illness."
- Chin: "This health anxiety feels overwhelming."
- Collarbone: "I'm afraid of what could happen."
- Under the Arm: "I can't stop worrying about my health."
- Top of the Head: "This anxiety is exhausting."

Affirmations (Second Round):
- Eyebrow: "I choose to trust my body's healing abilities."
- Side of the Eye: "I release my fear about my health."
- Under the Eye: "I am safe and healthy right now."
- Under the Nose: "I trust my body to take care of me."
- Chin: "I am calm, relaxed, and in balance."
- Collarbone: "I choose peace over anxiety."
- Under the Arm: "I am grateful for my body."

- Top of the Head: "I trust in my body's natural health."

5. Anxiety About Making Decisions

Set-Up Statement: (While tapping the karate chop point):

"Even though I feel anxious about making decisions and worry about making the wrong choice, I deeply and completely accept myself."

Tapping Sequence:
- Eyebrow: "I'm anxious about making decisions."
- Side of the Eye: "I'm afraid I'll make the wrong choice."
- Under the Eye: "This anxiety about deciding."
- Under the Nose: "It feels overwhelming."
- Chin: "I don't trust myself to make the right decision."
- Collarbone: "I feel so uncertain."
- Under the Arm: "I'm afraid of making a mistake."
- Top of the Head: "This decision-making anxiety."

Affirmations (Second Round):
- Eyebrow: "I trust myself to make the right decisions."
- Side of the Eye: "I release my fear of making mistakes."
- Under the Eye: "I trust my intuition and judgement."
- Under the Nose: "I am confident in my choices."
- Chin: "I can make decisions with ease."
- Collarbone: "I release my anxiety about this decision."
- Under the Arm: "I trust that I am on the right path."
- Top of the Head: "I feel calm and confident in my choices."

By following these set-up statements and affirmations through the tapping points, you will help your body and mind reduce anxiety and cultivate a sense of peace, calm, and emotional balance. Use these sequences whenever you feel anxious, and over time, you will notice a significant shift in how you respond to stressful situations.

1. Stress from Daily Responsibilities

For each tapping round, you will tap on the following points:

1. **Karate Chop** (side of the hand)
2. **Eyebrow** (beginning of the brow, near the nose)
3. **Side of the Eye** (on the bone beside the eye)
4. **Under the Eye** (on the bone beneath the eye)
5. **Under the Nose** (between the nose and upper lip)
6. **Chin** (in the crease below the bottom lip)
7. **Collarbone** (just below the collarbone)
8. **Under the Arm** (about four inches below the armpit)
9. **Top of the Head** (crown of the head)

Set-Up Statement: (While tapping the karate chop point):

> ✓ *"Even though I feel stressed by my daily responsibilities and everything I need to do, I deeply and completely accept myself."*

First Round: Addressing the Stress
- Eyebrow: "This stress from all my responsibilities."
- Side of the Eye: "I feel so overwhelmed."

- Under the Eye: "There's too much to do."
- Under the Nose: "I'm feeling the pressure."
- Chin: "It's hard to keep up."
- Collarbone: "I feel stressed and overburdened."
- Under the Arm: "There's just too much going on."
- Top of the Head: "This stress is exhausting."

Second Round: Releasing the Tension
- Eyebrow: "I'm ready to release this tension."
- Side of the Eye: "I choose to let go of this stress."
- Under the Eye: "I release the pressure to do everything."
- Under the Nose: "I am letting go of feeling overwhelmed."
- Chin: "I am allowing myself to relax."
- Collarbone: "I can let go of this burden."
- Under the Arm: "I am releasing this stress now."
- Top of the Head: "I feel lighter already."

Third Round: Affirming Peace and Calm
- Eyebrow: "I choose to feel calm and in control."
- Side of the Eye: "I trust that I can manage everything."
- Under the Eye: "I am relaxed and at ease."
- Under the Nose: "I can manage my responsibilities with ease."
- Chin: "I choose to stay calm no matter what."
- Collarbone: "I feel peaceful and grounded."
- Under the Arm: "I am in control and calm."
- Top of the Head: "I am calm, capable, and relaxed."

2. Stress About Work Deadlines

Set-Up Statement: (While tapping the karate chop point):

"Even though I'm stressed about all these work deadlines, I deeply and completely accept myself."
  First Round: Addressing the Stress
- Eyebrow: "This stress about my deadlines."
- Side of the Eye: "I'm worried I won't get it all done."
- Under the Eye: "There's too much pressure at work."

More en Volume 2

Final Thoughts

You now have everything you need to embark on a new chapter of your life one where you are empowered to manifest your deepest desires, free from the emotional and mental blocks that once held you back. Tapping offers you the key to emotional freedom, and the Law of Attraction provides the framework for turning your dreams into reality. Together, these tools will support you as you continue to grow, evolve, and create a life filled with joy, abundance, love, and success.

As you continue your journey, remember to be patient with yourself, trust in your own power, and remain open to the infinite possibilities that await you. Your manifestation journey has only just begun, and the future is full of exciting potential.

Embrace it fully.

Final Reflections:

Continuing Your Manifestation Journey

Now that you have explored the vast potential of tapping and the Law of Attraction, you are standing at the doorway of a new, empowered way of living. This is not just about manifesting isolated goals it is about transforming your entire approach to life. Through tapping, you have learned how to release emotional blocks, align your energy, and focus on what you truly desire, but most importantly, you have gained the tools to make this a lifelong practice of growth and self-empowerment.

As you move forward, there are a few final reflections that can help you stay grounded in your practice and continue evolving on your journey.

1. The Power of Small Steps

Transformation does not always come from huge leaps forward; often, it is the small, consistent steps that create the most lasting change. Each tapping session, each moment of emotional release, and each affirmation you speak brings you closer to the life you want to create. Trust the process and know that even on days when the progress feels slow, you are still moving in the right direction.

Every day offers you a chance to take one small step closer to your dreams, whether it is through a quick tapping session, a moment of gratitude, or simply being more mindful of your thoughts and emotions. These small actions, when repeated over time, have the power to bring about incredible change.

2. Honour Your Emotional Journey

Throughout this book, you have learned to tap into your emotions—both positive and negative. It is important to remember that your emotions are not your enemy, even when they are uncomfortable. They are signals, guiding you to areas that need attention, healing, and transformation.

Honour the emotions that come up, even if they seem difficult. Use tapping to work through them rather than pushing them aside. The more you allow yourself to process your feelings, the more you will free up emotional energy for positive change.

3. Stay Open to Growth

The principles of tapping and the Law of Attraction are not static they are part of a living, evolving process. As you continue to grow, your desires, beliefs, and goals will naturally evolve as well. Stay open to this growth. What you want today may shift as you move forward on your journey, and that is perfectly okay.

Growth means being willing to change your perspective, try new things, and let go of what no longer serves you. As you evolve, tapping will continue to be a powerful tool to help you navigate this change, allowing you to stay aligned with your true self and your ever-expanding potential.

4. Share Your Journey

One of the most rewarding aspects of working with tapping and the Law of Attraction is that it not only transforms your life, but it also has the potential to inspire and uplift those around you. As you experience the benefits of this practice, consider sharing your journey with others. Whether you teach someone the basics of tapping or simply share your personal story, you may inspire someone else to begin their own path of healing and manifestation.

Sometimes, we learn the most by teaching or sharing our experiences. By explaining your process, offering encouragement, or simply being open about the changes you have experienced, you not only help others but also reinforce your own growth and understanding.

5. Embrace the Infinite Possibilities

The Law of Attraction teaches us that the universe is full of infinite possibilities. What you can manifest in your life is limited only by the boundaries you set in your mind. As you continue your journey, remember that there is always more available to you more abundance, more love, more success, more joy.

When doubts arise, use tapping to release them, and remind yourself that you can achieve far more than you can currently imagine. Your dreams can expand and grow beyond what you thought possible, and the universe is always ready to support you when you are in alignment with your desires.

6. Celebrate Your Wins Big and Small

Remember to give yourself credit for your accomplishments along the way. Every victory is worth celebrating, whether it takes the form of a major manifestation like a new job or relationship or a more subtle change like feeling more at ease or confident. These victories provide you a boost and serve as a reminder that you are headed in the correct direction.

Additionally, celebrating helps you keep a mood of joy and thankfulness, which enhances your vibratory frequency and draws more good things into your life. Spend some time appreciating and acknowledging every step you take towards your goals. This will help to strengthen the emotional and energetic alignment that enables manifestation.

Moving Forward: The Path Ahead

Remember that you can design the life you want as you continue from this point on. You are equipped to conquer obstacles, cut self-limiting ideas, and align yourself with your goals. You can apply the methods in this book whenever you need them, whether they involve tapping, visualisation, meditation, or creating affirmations.

The manifestation journey is a continuous process that offers chances for development, learning, and evolution. Moments of great accomplishment and happiness will coexist with periods of difficulty and introspection. You will always be able to manage these situations with poise, fortitude, and self-compassion if tapping is a regular part of your routine.

Keep in mind that you are creating a life that is profoundly in line with your true self, not merely goals. You are getting closer to your greatest potential with each thought, feeling, and deed, and by being dedicated to your practice, you are creating the opportunity for an infinitely bright future.

Final Words of Encouragement

Believe in yourself and your ability to bring about positive change in your life as you go ahead on your manifestation journey. You have already gone a long way, and there are still plenty of chances for development, change, and fulfilment on the road ahead.

Have faith in the cosmos, in yourself, and in the process. You can create the life of your desires if you have tapping and the Law of Attraction on your side. Remain focused, keep moving forward, and never forget that you already have all you want.

Now that you have the tools, you may move through your manifestation path with joy, clarity, and confidence. It is a beautiful, continuous process.

You have got this. Embrace it fully, and watch your dreams unfold.

Conclusion

As the journey comes to an end, it is critical to consider the main takeaways presented in this book. Discovering the potential of **Emotional Freedom Technique (EFT)** and how it works in combination with **manifestation** has given you access to skills that can change your perspective, let go of limiting beliefs, and open the door to attracting the life you want.

You now know how to utilise tapping to break through emotional blocks, deal with stress, and change deeply rooted patterns related to relationships, money, and self-worth. The detailed instructions have given you easy methods to rewire your mind for success and plenty and access your emotional freedom.

Remember that **consistency** is the key to true transformation. You can feel more empowered, have more clarity, and release emotions by continuing your tapping exercise. You make room for fresh possibilities and fulfilling experiences to enter your life every time you confront and overcome a limiting idea or emotional block.

Implementing these action steps into practice has many benefits, including reduced stress, a more abundant attitude, improved relationships, and more self-confidence. You are capable and have the resources to create the life you want. Moving on and realising your dreams is now your responsibility.

Thank you for allowing us to be a part of your tapping and Law of Attraction journey with this book. I hope it serves as a reminder and a roadmap to help you draw in all the success, happiness, and wealth you are due in life.

Bibliography

Choosing Therapy strives to provide our readers with mental health content that is correct and actionable. I have high standards for what can be cited within our articles. Acceptable sources include government agencies, universities and colleges, scholarly journals, industry and professional associations, and other high-integrity sources of mental health journalism.

- Stapleton, P. Crighton, G., Sabot, D., & O'Neill, H.M. (2020). Re-examining the effect of emotional freedom techniques on stress biochemistry: A randomized controlled trial. Psychological Trauma: Theory, Research, Practice, and Policy, 12(8), 869-877. 10.1037/tra0000563

- Bach, D., Groesbeck, G, Stapleton, P, Sims, R., Blickheuser, K., & Church, D., (2019). Clinical EFT (Emotional freedom techniques) improves multiple physiological markers of health. Journal of Evidence Based Integrative Medicine, 24. https://doi.org/10.1177/2515690X18823691

- Chatwin, H., Stapleton, P., Porter, B., Devine, S., & Sheldon, T. (2016). The effectiveness of cognitive behavioural therapy and emotional freedom techniques in reducing depression and anxiety among adults: A pilot study. The Journal of Integrative Medicine, 15(2), 27-34.

- Church, D. & Brooks, A.J. (2010). The effect of a brief emotional freedom techniques self-intervention on anxiety, depression, pain, and cravings in health care workers. The Journal of Integrative Medicine, 9(5), 40-43. https://doi.org/10.1016/j.explore.2020.11.012

- Gaesser, A.H. & Karan, O.C. (2017). A randomized controlled comparison of emotional freedom technique and cognitive-behavioural therapy to reduce adolescent anxiety: A pilot study. The Journal of Alternative and Complementary Medicine, 23(2), 102.108. 10.1089/acm.2015.0316

- Patterson, S.L. (2016). The effect of emotional freedom technique on stress and anxiety in nursing students: A pilot study. Nurse Education Today, 40, 104-110. 10.1016/j.nedt.2016.02.003

- Nelms, J.A. & Castel, L. (2016). A systematic review and meta-analysis of randomized and nonrandomized trials of clinical emotional freedom techniques (EFT) for the treatment of depression. Explore: The Journal of Science and Healing, 12(6), 416-426. https://doi.org/10.1016/j.explore.2016.08.001

- Brattberg, G. (2008). Self-administered EFT (Emotional freedom techniques) in individuals with fibromyalgia: A randomized trial. The Journal of Integrative Medicine, 7(4), 30-35.

- Bougea, A.M., Spandideas, N., Alexopoulos, E.C., Thomaides, T., Chrousos, G.P., & Darviri, C. (2013). Effect of the emotional freedom technique on perceived stress, quality of life, and cortisol salivary levels in tension-type headache. Explore: The Journal of Science and Healing, 9(2), 91-99. https://doi.org/10.1016/j.explore.2012.12.005

- Padmapriya, D. & Jenifer, B.S. (2020). Effectiveness of emotional freedom technique tapping and acupressure on post-operative pain reduction among post-operative clients. Journal of Pharmacy Research, 14(7), 1046-1050.

- Connolly, S. & Sakai, C. (2011). Brief trauma intervention with Rwandan genocide-survivors using thought field therapy. International Journal of Emergency Mental Health, 13(3), 161–172.

- Geronilla, L., Minewiser, L. Mollon, P., McWilliams, M. & Clond, M. (2016). EFT (emotional freedom techniques) remediates PTSD and psychological symptoms in veterans: A randomized controlled replication trial. >Energy Psychology, 8(2), 29-41. 10.9769/EPJ.2016.8.2. LG
- Salas, M.M. Brooks, A.J. & Rowe, J.E. (2011). The immediate effect of a brief energy psychology intervention (emotional freedom techniques) on specific phobias: A pilot study. Explore: The Journal of Science and Healing, 7(3), 155-161. https://doi.org/10.1016/j.explore.2011.02.005

- Wells, S. Polglase, K. Andrews, H.B., Carrington, P, & Baker, A.H. (2003). Evaluation of a meridian-based intervention, emotional freedom techniques (EFT), for reducing specific phobias of small animals. Journal of Clinical Psychology, 59(9), 943-966. https://doi.org/10.1002/jclp.10189

- Sezgin, N. & Ozcan, B. (2009). The effect of progressive muscular relaxation and emotional freedom techniques on test anxiety in high school students: A randomized controlled trial. Energy Psychology, 1(1). 10.9769/EPJ.2009.1.1. NS

- Dincer, B. & Inangil, D. (2021). The effect of emotional freedom techniques on nurses' stress, anxiety, and burnout levels during the COVID-19 pandemic: A randomized controlled trial. Explore: The Journal of Science and Healing, 17(2), 109-114. https://doi.org/10.1016/j.explore.2020.11.012
- Your Voice Matters

Acknowledgments

Without the encouragement and support of many amazing people, this book would not have been possible, and I am incredibly appreciative of their efforts.

I want to start by expressing my gratitude to my husband, Fernando, whose unalterable belief in me has served as a continual source of motivation. I sincerely could not have finished this project without your help, and your encouragement, tolerance, and advice have meant the world to me.

To Susana Aguire, your wise counsel and helpful criticism during the writing process influenced the development of this book into what it is now. I appreciate the time and work you put into reading drafts and imparting your knowledge.

I would especially like to thank my family, who have always been my biggest supporters: Maria Angela, Maria Clara, Alexandra, Juan, Daniel, Carmen, Amanda, Jordi, and my grandson Hugo. Even when the path became difficult, your love, compassion, and unwavering support gave me the willpower and inspiration to keep going.

I want to express my gratitude to everyone in my life for their support and for always being there to listen when I needed it. I appreciate your patience when I lost myself in the writing process, and your confidence in my work kept me inspired.

Lastly, I would want to express my gratitude to the readers for their confidence and interest. In your own path, I hope this book will be helpful and inspirational.

This project has been an act of love, and I owe a debt of gratitude to everyone who helped make it a reality.

About the Author

Marilena Mocanu is a passionate advocate of emotional healing, personal development, and the transformational potential of mindfulness exercises like Emotional Freedom Technique (EFT). With training in holistic therapy, coaching, psychology, spirituality, and manifestation, she has devoted her professional life to helping others in overcoming emotional obstacles and limiting beliefs to lead more satisfying lives.

Both her educational achievements and years of real-world experience dealing with people looking to advance both personally and professionally have contributed to Marilena's extensive understanding of affirmations. She has worked with top authorities in mindset coaching and emotional wellness, which has improved her ability to help people navigate the challenges of financial independence and emotional well-being.

In addition to publishing **The Path to Prosperity** and **The Magic Words "I AM,"** Marilena continues to offer insightful perspectives on abundance, motivation, and personal growth. She focusses on giving people the tools they need to realise their full potential and overcome stress, self-doubt, and financial limitations.

Marilena likes to travel, do yoga, meditate, and spend time with her family in London when she is not writing or working with clients.

Marilena Mocanu's writing stands for her strong commitment to individual empowerment and development, and she is committed to inspiring others to reach emotional freedom and live the life they want.

I would like to inform you that a part of the revenues from the sale of this book will be donated to schools in Romania, Spain, and the United Kingdom helping to ensure that children receive at least one nutritious meal each day.

Sincerely, Marilena Mocanu

Associated Books
May you be interested??

ASIN : B0CPBV6Q5W
Publisher : Independently published
Language : Spanish
Paperback : 123 pages
ISBN-13 : 979-8968273205

ASIN : B0CNWJHCQ25
Publisher : Independently published
Language : English
Paperback : 123 pages
ISBN-13 : 979-8867418472

ASIN : B0DJDBBF5Y
Publisher : Independently published
Language : English
Paperback : 249 pages
ISBN-13 : 979-8340871091

ASIN : B0DKXVGRCH
Publisher : Independently published
Language : Spanish
Paperback : 265 pages
ISBN-13 : 979-8342491433